KT-561-624

In memory of Tom,
who gave me the encouragement
and confidence to write this book.
Also to Ted who helped me to get through
the hardest years.

Table of Contents

GLOSSARY OF TERMINOLOGY

CAO	Central applications system for universities, institutes of technology and other colleges.
DAI	Dyslexia Association of Ireland.
DIT	Dublin Institute of Technology comprising the College of Commerce, Aungier Street; Colleges of Technology, Kevin Street and Bolton Street; College of Marketing and Design, Mountjoy Square, College of Catering, Cathal Brugha Street and the College of Music.
ESRI	Economic and Social Research Institute.
FETAC	Further Education and Training Awards Council.
HETAC	Higher Education and Training Awards Council.
IATI	Institute of Accounting Technicians of Ireland.
LCA	Leaving Certificate Applied.
LCV	Leaving Certificate Vocational.
NEPS	National Educational Psychological Service.
NCI	National College of Ireland.
NFQ	National Framework of Qualifications
NLN	National Learning Network
NUI	National University of Ireland, comprising of UCD, University College, Dublin, UCC, University College, Cork, UCG, University College, Galway, St. Patrick's College, Maynooth.
NCAD	National College of Art and Design.
PLC	Post Leaving Certificate Courses.
SESS	Special Education Support Service
UCAS	Centralised application system for degree and diploma courses in the U.K.

Introduction

The origins of this book lie in the journey of discovery I have taken since 1985 when it was confirmed that our twin sons, Robin and Simon, had a learning difficulty. It was a journey that began in ignorance. In spite of the fact that I was a secondary teacher, I knew little about the subject of dyslexia at that time. Although I received help from teachers, psychologists and DAI, (the Dyslexia Association of Ireland), it was a journey taken for the most part on my own as I tried, over the years, to assess what exactly were the twins' difficulties, what techniques worked best for them and what resources were available to them. In recent years I have met with parents soon after a child was similarly diagnosed and have heard the same questions being asked and have seen these parents starting out on the same path searching for the same information.

My primary objective in writing this book is a hope that it will be a source of relevant and practical information for parents of children with dyslexia.

At the time the twins were diagnosed, I was fortunate in that I was working as a guidance counsellor, as indeed, I still am. My role as a guidance counsellor puts me in a central place in the school system where I had access to information relevant to their needs. I deal with the vocational, educational and personal counselling needs of students from the ages of twelve to eighteen. I am involved, among other things, as a member of a team looking after the needs of students with diverse learning difficulties. I receive copies of psycho-educational assessment reports on such students. In cases where students appear to have learning difficulties, I suggest referral for assessment to their parents. I keep up-to-date with the trends in employment and educational courses available after second-level.

This is a rapidly changing field with more flexibility entering into the routes to qualifications. This flexibility can be particularly important for students with dyslexia. Up to 2001 I was also a subject teacher of Business and English. However since then I have been involved in teaching students with special educational needs. During the years my roles, as a teacher, a guidance counsellor and more recently as a resource teacher, have been of great benefit to the twins and the corollary of this is that I have become much more aware of dyslexia and the difficulties that students with dyslexia face in second-level education. These difficulties are shared by students with other hidden learning difficulties such as Dyspraxia, Asperger's Syndrome and Attention Deficit Disorder.

A second objective in writing this book is to increase the awareness of the needs of such students in the public mind and, in particular, the teaching profession. While there has been some progress in recent years, much more is needed. I have personally known many students who were not diagnosed until their mid-teens. They had passed through primary school and partially through second-level without teachers picking up their difficulties and advising an assessment. Certainly they have met with failure and their confidence and self-esteem have been affected greatly by such a late diagnosis.

During much of the time that I have been involved with DAI, campaigning as a member of the Association for more resources and more teacher training on the topic of learning difficulties, very little changed. This was reflected in the first edition of this book in 1998. However since then there have been developments which hopefully will lead to better provision for students with learning difficulties in Irish education. These include the establishment of the National Educational Psychological Service (NEPS) and the Special Education Support Service (SESS), the Report of the Task Force on Dyslexia, the Education Act 1998, the Education (Welfare) Act 2000 and the Education of Persons with Special Needs Act 2004.

I will be referring to the twins, Robin and Simon, and the techniques which worked for them and some that did not throughout this book, so it may be helpful to give a brief introduction to them, our family history and to explain how the dyslexia has affected them.

They were our first children and were already showing some signs of difficulty at the age of two. They were slow to talk. We attributed some of this to 'Twintalk', which is that they were so busy communicating between themselves that it slowed down their language development. At a later stage they mispronounced words. They also found sequences difficult to remember and they tended to be clumsy. They did not tie shoelaces until they were nine and they rode a bicycle for the first time at the age of ten. In their early years at school they found order and pattern difficult and they repeated a year. As they had started school at four years and ten months, this made them old for their class.

On the basis of a psycho-educational assessment, we were fortunate to get two places in St. Oliver Plunkett's School in Monkstown when they were eight. St. Oliver Plunkett's is a primary school which was established to provide specialised tuition for pupils who have reading difficulties. The twins spent two years there. They went back into fourth class in Carysfort National School but, since their reading was still three to four years behind, they had considerable difficulties with the primary school curriculum. We applied for and received an exemption from Irish from the Department of Education and Science. This helped. It had been hard to see them struggling to learn the sounds in English and then having to learn different sounds for the same letters in Irish. During the years in Carysfort National School they attended the DAI Saturday morning classes and also attended summer school. It is much to their credit that they tackled all this extra work with perseverance. Towards the end of their years in primary school, their reading developed and this opened the way to making progress in school.

After much research about second-level schools, we decided to send them to St. Gerard's, Bray, for their secondary schooling. Here, provided they received help at home with notes for the different subjects, they coped well. As this was one of the early years of the Junior Certificate course, there were no revision handbooks available, so it was a question of summarising the books ourselves. For the first time they were participating fully in class and received great affirmation when they passed class exams and tests.

They continued to need help with notes during the three years of the Junior Certificate course and also needed help with goal-setting and organisation of work. They attended the examination preparation classes run by the DAI. They both were delighted to receive three honours grades on higher level papers in the Junior Certificate and good passes in their other subjects. This gave an enormous boost to their confidence and it showed how far they had journeyed since learning to read at the age of eleven.

They sat their Leaving Certificate in 1998. They took their subjects at Ordinary level. Their results were mainly B's, with one 'A' and inevitably both received a 'D' in English. Robin went to the National College of Ireland to study for a National Certificate in Computing. This was much more suited to his abilities than the Leaving Certificate which has so much verbal content. He achieved a Merit grade and proceeded on to Dundalk Institute of Technology to do a National Diploma. He is now working in the computer industry. Simon has completed the Accounting Technician qualification with IATI and is now working in the public service.

They still have difficulties with spelling. I can never see them spelling well but they use a word-processor with a spell-check competently.

During these years my husband, Tom, and myself decided early on that I was more suited to work with the twins as I am a teacher. Part of the reason I was able to work with the boys is their co-operative and pleasant personalities and their desire to achieve. Together we formed a very compatible work team (for the most part). At times progress was infuriatingly slow; at times impatience set in. I learnt to recognise when, as a result of being too tired, I became more edgy and far more critical. A difficulty which might have been laughed at in September could be the basis for a row in February when we were much more fatigued. I learnt to deliberately avoid confronting issues when under stress. To give out about schoolwork on some occasions would be detrimental to the other work we had put in on self-esteem and confidence. We wanted Robin and Simon to feel home was a refuge and that our love was not conditional on school performance.

Together as a family we have shared moments of great exhilaration and satisfaction at their achievements, such as their Junior and Leaving Certificate results, doing An Gaisce Awards at bronze and silver level, their participation in the Young Scientist Competition and of course, when they both graduated from their chosen courses at third-level.

Because there was a gap of six years between the twins and their brother Tom, it meant we were able to give them more attention than might be possible in a family situation where the siblings are closer together in age. It also meant they had very little competition inside the family. In some families it can increase pressure on the student with dyslexia when younger brothers and sisters overtake their achievements in school tasks such as reading and writing. Soon after Tom died in infancy, the youngest member of the family, Ted, was born in 1986. We were conscious of the fact that dyslexia can run in families and had become aware of adult members in the family who have dyslexic characteristics.

From the beginning we had been on the look-out for indicators that Ted might be dyslexic but because he was a very articulate, logical child with good co-ordination, we had felt there was no problem. However, by first class, we discovered he was memorising the content of his readers, so it appeared as though he could read but in reality he had no grasp of reading. He was assessed by a psychologist and his results showed an uneven profile of ability with exceptional strengths in the logical and mathematical areas, average ability in verbal skills and below average in spelling. He received intensive remedial intervention and it had dramatic effects. There is a residual spelling difficulty. Learning Irish and other languages was hard work. However with minimal supports at second level such as appropriate subject choice and an exemption from the third language, he achieved well and is now doing engineering at university. He is a good example of how early intervention can minimise the effects of dyslexia in some students.

During these years we have spent many hundreds of pounds, if not thousands of pounds, on the three boys. Assessments and extra tuition are major costs. This experience is mirrored by many families who have had to fund the necessary assessments and extra tuition costs. These were the fortunate students. There are many cases where families do not have the necessary resources to help the child.

We realise we have been fortunate in benefiting from the support services which were provided by the Department of Education and Science. Robin and Simon received on-going learning support help in school; they went to St. Oliver Plunkett's School in Monkstown for two years; they received an exemption from Irish from fourth class on and they had reasonable accommodation in state examinations. Not all students with dyslexia have the same access to such facilities. Because they did the Leaving Certificate in 1998, their certificate does not have an explanatory note stating they did not participate in some element of the exam. Such an explanatory note is put on the results of students who avail of reasonable accommodation in state exams since 2000.

Over the years we have received great help. Between the three boys they have attended the following schools and colleges:

♦ Mount Anville National School, Kilmacud.
♦ St. Oliver Plunkett's School, Monkstown.
♦ Carysfort National School, Blackrock.
♦ Scoil San Treasa, Mount Merrion.
♦ St. Gerard's School, Bray.
♦ National College of Ireland.
♦ Dundalk Institute of Technology.
♦ Dun Laoghaire Senior College.
♦ Institute of Accounting Technicians of Ireland.
♦ University College Dublin.

The staffs of all these institutions have always been most co-operative and positive and have done their utmost to meet their needs. They have listened and tried to facilitate our requests. Our thanks to all the teachers and staff concerned. In particular thanks are due to the Headmaster and staff of St. Gerard's School where all three completed their second-level education.

DAI has been an invaluable source of information. The newsletters and lectures have helped us to understand dyslexia, how it affects students and how to help them cope. I have attended their lectures and conferences. Over the years the twins have attended their Saturday School and exam preparation classes. Parents of children with learning difficulties should become members of this organisation. It is a great support to talk to other parents of dyslexic students, to share information and to feel that one is not struggling alone.

My colleagues in St. David's Secondary School, Greystones, have given me great advice and instructed me in their own particular subjects so that I could help with the twins' homework, as well as listening and giving me constant encouragement.

Much thanks are due to a number of friends, Pamela McAree and Donal Lynch, who did trojan work editing this manuscript and my colleagues, Cairbre O Ciardha, Siobhán Connaughton and Deirdre McElroy, who gave me advice and suggestions.

I hope that my book will pass on some of the insights I have gained and that it will help students with dyslexia, their parents and their teachers to understand how dyslexia can affect students at second-level and what can be done to help them overcome their difficulties. I also hope that it might raise public awareness. If teachers, parents and the general public are more aware that such problems exist, it will lead to earlier identification and to more facilities and support systems being provided.

Dyslexia at Second-Level and Beyond

2

My knowledge about dyslexia results from my own practical experience as a teacher, a guidance counsellor and, most important of all, a parent. From the time my husband and I became aware that Robin and Simon had a learning difficulty, I have read many books and attended courses to further my knowledge. So when I describe dyslexia it is with knowledge gleaned from the books I have read, from seminars I have attended and from practical experience in the school and at home.

While I try to give an overall description of dyslexia, I am looking in particular at the way dyslexia can affect a student at second-level. This is the sector of education in which I work and have experience.

Dyslexia is diagnosed by an educational psychologist who identifies marked under-achievement in language skills in comparison with a student's level of intelligence. The word itself comes from the Greek meaning 'difficulty with words or language'. International figures show it occurs in about 4% to 8% of the population in varying degrees and with varying effects. Dyslexic difficulties can occur along a continuum from mild to severe. Ability also occurs along a continuum from superior ability to average, below average and extends into general learning difficulties. The dyslexia continuum and the ability continuum are not correlated. It is possible for a child with superior ability to have severe dyslexia, or a child with mild learning difficulties to have these difficulties compounded by mild dyslexia.

When the Task Force on Dyslexia, set up by the Minister for Education and Science, published its Report in July 2001, it defined dyslexia as follows:

'*Dyslexia is manifested in a continuum of specific learning difficulties related to the acquisition of basic skills in reading, spelling and/or writing, such difficulties being unexpected in relation to an individual's other abilities and educational experiences. Dyslexia can be described at the neurological, cognitive and behavioural levels. It is typically characterised by inefficient information processing, including difficulties in phonological processing, working memory, rapid naming and automaticity of basic skills. Difficulties in organisation, sequencing and motor skills may also be present.*'

Dyslexia is not related to low intelligence. Generally it is true to say that intelligence and reading ability are strongly linked. Students with dyslexia are different. Intelligence and language skills are not correlated for them. There are plenty of cases of students with very high IQ scores who had difficulty in written language skills. Some of the historical figures of which this was true are Einstein, Edison, Yeats, Leonardo Da Vinci and Rodin.

While psychologists are not sure as to the causes of dyslexia, there is evidence of a genetic component. In March 1996 I attended the AGM of the Dyslexia Association of Ireland, at which Mr. T. Pottage from the British Dyslexia Association spoke on the advantages of computers for dyslexics. Mr. Pottage, who has a dyslexic son, made the comment that dyslexia is often inherited. Parents inherit it from their children! It is only since his son was diagnosed that he has recognised some of the effects of dyslexia in himself. The same is true of myself. I had no problems at school and went on to third-level education. However now I recognise that I do have some difficulties. I can never tell right from left and I transpose letters and numbers. My own family history would lend itself to the argument that there is a genetic component in dyslexia. My brother was diagnosed as dyslexic in his mid-teens and my three sons are all affected to some extent. Robin and Simon would lend even stronger evidence to a genetic component. They are identical twins and, in their difficulties with languages, have mirrored each other. At the time they were learning to read, they made exactly the same mistakes. 'Saw' became 'was' and 'on' became 'no' for both of them. Even now, when writing, they make similar spelling mistakes. If there is a history of dyslexia in a family, parents should be on the look-out for indicators that a child may be affected. The earlier the child gets help, the less the damage to self-esteem.

Happily there are now screening tests which can point to possible difficulties for the child from the age of four. The DEST (Dyslexia Early Screening Test) and DST (Dyslexia Screening Test) have been developed at the University of Sheffield and trials of these tests have been held by the Psychology Department in Trinity College, Dublin. The DST is designed for use with students from 6 years and 6 months to the age of 16 years and 5 months. The tests are available from ETC Consult.

CoPS (Cognitive Profiling System) is a computer based test to screen for dyslexic characteristics in the four to six age group. It was developed at the University of Hull. It measures the child's reaction to various challenges on a computer screen. It has been updated and now has four programmes:

- CoPSbaseline for children between four and five and six months.
- LucidCoPS for children between four and eight.
- LASS Junior for children between eight and eleven.
- LASS Secondary for children between eleven and fifteen.

Up until the development of these screening tests, the earliest a child would be assessed was at age seven or eight. The reason for the assessment would be worries over the child's achievement in school. The child would already be failing. If screening tests can point to dyslexia at the age of four or five, before the child has fallen behind, help can be given earlier and the difficulty may not become so acute. Importantly, if children have to wait until seven or eight to be diagnosed and are already falling behind, self-esteem is already being affected. This compounds the difficulties. Afraid of appearing to fail they can become experts in avoiding tasks that they do badly. Evasion tactics used may include psychosomatic illnesses, acting up, tantrums or becoming the class clown. They can give up trying, as it can be preferable to fail by not working at a subject rather than by not being able to do it. This is particularly relevant at second-level when the peer group is so important to the developing adolescent.

THE PSYCHO-EDUCATIONAL ASSESSMENT

Parents and/or teachers may voice concerns about a child's progress. Such concerns may be confirmed by the use of screening tests. However, to be able to make a positive diagnosis of dyslexia, it is necessary to have a psycho-educational assessment carried out by a suitably qualified psychologist. Such an assessment may be carried out through the school by a National Educational Psychological Service (NEPS) psychologist or parents may opt for a private assessment. Because of the long waiting time, many parents opt for private assessment, either with the Dyslexia Association of Ireland or with a psychologist in private practice. A list of the latter is available on the website of the Psychological Society of Ireland www.psihq.ie Private assessment costs from €400 to €600. Tax relief is available on the fees paid for private assessments. This is claimed by using the MED 1 form when completing year end tax returns. However if the assessment recommends extra tuition, the cost of this tuition cannot be claimed.

The assessment involving tests and observations lasts over two hours. There may be some brief oral feedback immediately after the assessment, but a report of the assessment will issue some time later. This is a detailed and important document. It will contain the following information:

♦ Name and address of student, date of birth, chronological age and date of assessment.

♦ Reasons for referral.

♦ Background information on the child such as developmental history, medical history and family history.

♦ A note of the tests used and results obtained. This explains the child's abilities and weaknesses and comments on the child's coping strategies.

♦ A conclusion based on the testing

♦ Recommendations on the type of help, teaching strategies and support services the child needs.

A main component of the testing is an intelligence test such as the Wechsler Intelligence Scale for children, 4th edition (WISC 4). The profile of a student with dyslexia on sub-tests of the WISC can show significant differences, indicating the child's strengths and weaknesses. Dr. Hornsby in her book *Overcoming Dyslexia* says 'Very significant clues for the diagnosis of dyslexia are the low scores on Digit Span and Coding tests. These indicate a lack of short-term memory for abstract symbols, shapes and numbers'. Other tests used could include Wechsler Individual Attainment Tests, 2nd. Edition (WIAT-11), tests of laterality and tests of visual and auditory memory, such as digit span, immediate visual recall, recall of designs, and fine motor and ocular motor control.

The report is an important document. It can be used by parents to help them understand the child's difficulties and to assist them in making informed educational choices. It will be referred to time and time again as the issues facing the child change. Because parents are the main decision-makers for the student, I have been surprised to discover occasions where they did not have access to a copy of the psychological report. Teachers also need a copy of the assessment as it should be used to work out teaching strategies for the child, based the child's strengths and weaknesses. Parents and/or primary level schools should ensure copies of all assessments are sent to the second-level school prior to the student entering first year. In the case of students receiving additional resource teaching at primary level, the second-level school needs the assessment in January prior to entrance as the requests for such additional teaching hours are made to the SENO (Special Educational Needs Organiser) in February. The report may be needed when applying for additional teaching help, exemptions from Irish or the third language requirement in NUI, support services at third-level, the provision of assistive technology or reasonable accommodation in state exams. A recent report, usually under two years old, is generally required for such applications.

Some parents fear that when students know they have dyslexia, the label will encourage them to do less as they have an excuse for not learning. I do not agree with this view. Many students feel a sense of relief. The diagnosis of dyslexia explains their lack of achievement in school and it can encourage them to make an effort provided the tasks are geared to their abilities. One student voiced his relief that there was 'nothing wrong in his head'. Another student in my own school was not diagnosed until he was fifteen. Up to this point he had been extremely disruptive and it was very likely he would be asked not to return to senior cycle. Once the diagnosis was made, he changed remarkably. He not only passed his Leaving Certificate, but also was in the running to be considered for Student of the Year at the end of his final year in the school.

There is research to show the dyslexic profile of abilities can contain strengths. Many of these students may be strong in logical reasoning which may lead to success in mastering computers. They may be good at constructional tasks such as building Lego or Meccano. Spatial Relations (the ability to visualise in three dimensions) can be a strength. In a video on dyslexia produced for the BBC programme QED, Tom West, an author who has written several books on dyslexia, suggests that dyslexia is a very positive asset in today's and tomorrow's world and that very good visual spatial skills may be more appropriate to a new world rather than the old skills based on words. Humdrum tasks such as spelling and sums can be left to computers. These were the skills of the medieval monks. Tom West has written a book called *In the Mind's Eye* which profiles a number of gifted individuals such as Faraday and Einstein, all of whom had some literacy or numeracy difficulties during their school career and later as adults.

DYSLEXIA AT SECOND-LEVEL

By the time they enter second-level, most students with dyslexia are able to read to some extent. If they have been lucky enough to be diagnosed early, they may have received some remedial/resource teaching. Some may have attended DAI workshops or have had extra tuition on a one-to-one basis. Indeed, if students cannot read by this stage, they will have major problems managing the second-level curriculum.

Many people believe that dyslexia is a problem with reading and that, if the student learns to read, the problem is solved. However it must be remembered the huge variety in the range and extent of the difficulties experienced by students with dyslexia. Each student has a unique profile of strengths and weaknesses. At second-level, students may experience difficulty in one or some of the following:

Reading

Most students with dyslexia will be able to read by the time they reach second-level. However the reading may be laboured or be affected by pressure of time or complicated texts. They can be slow at reading and can misread some words. They possibly confuse letters and sequences. They can concentrate so much on deciphering the text that they can lose comprehension. They may have to re-read a page to make sense of it. It can take them longer than other students to find a word or passage on a page. Even if they can read quite fluently, they may dislike reading aloud. In the pressure of an exam a student with dyslexia, who can read quite well, is quite liable to misread a question as stress can exacerbate dyslexic symptoms.

When students start at second-level their textbooks can be quite daunting. The texts are usually geared for the three years of the Junior Certificate course and many of the texts use the language suitable for students of fourteen or fifteen. This does not help students with dyslexia. They may find it difficult to pick out the main points and summarise the material in the textbooks. This skill is critical to success at second-level where students have to be familiar with so much information. Effective study technique requires students to be able to take notes of key points. They may also have difficulty when using reference material in picking out the relevant points they need and so become flooded with information.

Spelling

Whereas most students with dyslexia will have achieved some level of reading skills by the time of entry to second-level, spelling difficulties tend to persist for a longer period. Students with dyslexia may not perceive the sequences or patterns that letters make to form words. They may lack the visual memory of words. Many people spell well because they remember the visual shape of a word. They become aware if the word "looks" wrong. Students with dyslexia may not have this memory. Typical errors include:

- ♦ transposing letters, e.g. hostipal for hospital.
- ♦ letter confusion, d/b, p/q and m/w being mistaken for each other.

♦   omission of letters or endings e.g. spraind for sprained.

♦   phonetic spelling, e.g. kawphy for coffee, barax for barracks.

♦   impossible combinations of letters e.g. qiet.

♦   inconsistent spelling where the same word is spelt several ways.

♦   adding or deleting syllables or vowels, e.g. rember for remember.

If they take the time to try to spell correctly, it can slow down the writing process and interfere with the flow of ideas. Sometimes they try to avoid a word they cannot spell and seek an alternative. This can sound stilted and interrupts the flow of language. Some may mispronounce words and this can have dire consequences for spelling.

Handwriting

Handwriting can be difficult to read and badly formed. This may be the result of directional confusion and/or poor motor visual skills. Directional confusion affects concepts such as up/down, left/right or top/bottom. The student, when beginning to learn to write, does not know which way the pen should go. A video produced by the Eagle Hill School, Connecticut, tries to give parents, teachers and psychologists some insight into the difficulties faced by the student. There is an exercise to illustrate directional confusion. A mirror is set on a desk and a person is asked to copy a pattern but can look only into the reversed image on the mirror. Try this one out yourself and it will give you some appreciation of how difficult some students find the task of orientation. Another way to experience this is to turn the mouse of the computer upside down and to try to move the cursor on the screen. This may seem an extreme example. However when I first began to use the mouse, this is what I experienced for about a week until I learnt to make it an automatic task.

Note-taking

Many students with dyslexia face difficulties in taking notes either from the blackboard or in a lecture. Poor motor visual skills mean they find it difficult to combine looking at the board, copying into their notebook and then looking up to find the right place to continue. Visual memory problems mean they may take fewer words down from the board each time and so are looking back to the board more often. The writing on the board is likely to be in script handwriting which they may have difficulty deciphering.

In a lecture students with dyslexia may have to concentrate fully on what is being said in order to understand it. It is as though they have to translate it to make sense of it. The direct connection where a student can take down what a lecturer is saying and write simultaneously may not apply. This slows them down. If faced with words they cannot visualise and so cannot spell, they can come to a halt and so miss whatever is said next. Besides the problems of taking down notes, the finished copy is likely to be difficult to read and to study from because of poor handwriting and misspellings.

Presentation of Work

Their work can be difficult to correct because of poor handwriting, poor or bizarre spelling and lack of layout on the page. Spacing of work, margins and headings do not come naturally to some students with dyslexia. They can lose marks because teachers cannot decipher what they have written. It can also take far longer to correct. Teachers can sometimes judge students on the appearance of their work. If the work is very untidy and disorganised, assumptions may be made about the content with the consequence of lower marks.

Verbal expression

Some students with dyslexia have difficulty retrieving the correct name for a familiar object from memory. They know all about the object and what it does but the recall of the exact term eludes them. They may resort to terms like 'you know what I mean' or 'thingamijig'. When learning history, they may know the causes, course and results of an historical event such as the Reformation but the names of the people, events and places do not come to mind quickly. When attempting to explain something at length, they can lack organisation and structure. They may know what they want to say but they do not start with a beginning, go on to a middle and thence to a conclusion. It can be very mixed up.

Written Expression

While students with dyslexia may be familiar with a topic and have plenty of ideas, their written answers may lack planning and structure, so the points they wish to make are not clearly represented. Writing can be a cumbersome task and one which students may wish to avoid. Answers may be far too short and points may be left undeveloped. Sentence construction and punctuation can cause difficulties in clarity and precision of writing.

Sequencing

Sequencing plays a part in some of the other difficulties listed in this section. However it deserves to be mentioned separately because sequencing information is so important at second-level. Poor sequential skills may affect students in the following ways:

They may not perceive the day-to-day sequences that most people take for granted such as the days of the week or the months of the year. This can make planning homework and revision difficult. Teachers may feel they have communicated clear instructions to the class but students with dyslexia do not share the same concept of the time scale and so misinterpret what teachers have said. The structure of each day at second-level is not the same. Students may forget to do homework or take books in to school on the correct day.

If students are given a task of learning a sequence off-by-heart such as poetry or spellings, they may find it virtually impossible as they may confuse the sequence. With a lot of effort, it might be learnt in the evening, but is forgotten by the following morning. For this reason some students may find it difficult to tell jokes. They can mix-up the punchline and ruin the joke. If this happens with jokes, how much more difficult is it to learn a long poem?

When given a question either orally or in writing, they may find it difficult to sequence answers. This can mean that although they may know a lot of information, they cannot find the means to express it in a clearly structured way.

Maths

In Maths students with dyslexia may have difficulty in remembering sequences such as tables which can slow down calculations or the sequence of the steps to be followed in a long question. They may also take longer to distinguish between symbols such as + (plus) and x (multiply) or < (less than) and > (greater than). They may not grasp the distinction between words with exact meanings such as minus, subtraction and reduction. Small link words, which the student may overlook, can change the meaning of an instruction leaving the student confused, e.g. six <u>by</u> six, six <u>times</u> six, six <u>into</u> six, six sixes, six <u>plus</u> six and six <u>and</u> six. In a verbally expressed question it may be the English in the question and not the mathematical concept that they do not understand. In Maths the student usually works from right to left, which is opposite to the way words are read. This all adds to the difficulties. Poor layout and presentation can mean answers are wrong even if the method is correct. In an oral test students may need to decode the question to understand what they are being asked to do and so they miss the next question and fall behind. One student described a tables test at primary level by saying 'By the time I saw the numbers in my mind, and wrote the answer, I had missed the next question'. This student needed time to visualise and process the question.

Directional Confusion

This has been mentioned under handwriting but it can affect students with dyslexia in other aspects of the school curriculum. They may find it difficult to tell left from right, read maps, have difficulty finding their way about and remembering routes. In Physical Education or in other subjects where they have to follow a certain action, they may have to translate the action into instructions in their mind as to what their limbs should do. They do not automatically know which arm or leg to use. Frequently the teacher teaches by example. If the teacher is facing the students, when doing an action, it can confuse the student because it is the mirror image of what the student should do.

Following Instructions

The student with dyslexia may have difficulty following verbal instructions if more than one instruction is given at a time, particularly if direction or sequences are included. If the teacher gives an instruction such as 'When you have finished your work, and taken down your homework from the board, you may leave', the student may register the last phrase and leave immediately. This can lead to trouble in school.

Orally given details of school events may lack some essential detail by the time it reaches home and parents. An example may be the notice about a Parents' Night Meeting. By the time it reaches home, the date or the time or the venue may have been forgotten or confused.

Lack of Confidence

The student with dyslexia may experience a few or many of the difficulties mentioned above. However a very common by-product of having dyslexia is lack of confidence or low self-esteem. Students have experienced failure from an early age in a very public arena. They are aware that they do not make the same progress as their peers. It can make them reluctant to ask questions in class. They try to avoid answering questions in case the answer they give is wrong. Reading aloud can be embarrassing. They may face frustration in not being able to do tasks set by the teacher. Being in a classroom may be a source of anxiety and tension to them. They may avoid new challenges so as to avoid further failure. They may lack the confidence in their ability to achieve and may even give up trying. They may be embarrassed by their problem and be reluctant to tell other students that they are dyslexic. Under stress, such as in an exam, dyslexic characteristics can be exacerbated and tasks, previously managed well, become more difficult. This lack of confidence can permeate the whole of schooling and may even affect sports, hobbies, social relationships and career. This is the most damaging side effect of dyslexia in my opinion.

Again it must be stressed that each student with dyslexia is affected in varying ways. Some may have reading and spelling problems, for others it may be sequencing and structure. Some may be affected minimally, others severely. Teachers and school authorities need to know the profile of the individual student. The psycho-educational assessment gives valuable information and suggestions. Parents should be consulted and listened to. They have the inside track on the difficulties faced by the student and may have ideas on what strategies work best.

ALTERNATIVE THERAPIES

In the booklet *All Children Learn Differently, a Parent's Guide to Dyslexia* published by DAI, the Association advocates direct teaching as the optimum way of improving literacy skills. Teaching is time-consuming and often tedious, but when intervention in the form of appropriate teaching begins early in life and has the moral and practical support of home and school, it is successful. The Dyslexia Association's years of experience and knowledge of dyslexia has led it to the conclusion that there is no quick fix, no magic pill, no universal panacea which will provide a cure.

There have been many therapies put forward that claim to cure, prevent or have a positive effect on learning difficulties. Parents and professionals should watch out for any promoted method or product that costs a lot of money and promises an easy or quick 'cure'. Any method or product should be considered controversial and suspect if

♦ There is no research to prove it works.

♦ The research has not been independently replicated.

♦ The claims of the method or product far exceed the research results.

♦ The only proof is the personal testimony of parents or their children.

Before signing any contract, agreeing to any treatment or purchasing any product that sound too good to be true, ask to see the independent research papers that support the claims made on behalf of the product. Also ask professionals in the field about the method.

The Task Force on Dyslexia recommended that the Department of Education and Science commission a review of existing research on the effectiveness of such therapies and interventions.

Some non-teaching strategies for children with dyslexia include:

♦ Brain Gym. This is part of the Educational Kinesiology process. Kinesiology is the science of body movement and the relationships of muscles and posture to brain function. Further information is available from the Educational Kinesiology Foundation. Website: www.brainwise.co.uk

♦ Neuro-Physiological Theory. The term Neuro-Developmental Delay describes the omission or arrest of a stage in early development. Every normal baby, born at full term is born with a set of primitive reflexes (sometimes known as "survival reflexes"), which are inhibited or controlled by higher centres in the brain during the first year of life. If these are not inhibited at the correct time, they remain "active" in the body, and can interfere with motor control, eye functioning, eye-hand co-ordination and perceptual skills. The Institute of Neuro-Developmental Therapists. Website: www.inpp.org.uk

♦ Primary Movement. Primary Movement is a programme which seeks to replicate the early movements of the fetus and to enhance the maturation of the central nervous system. Website: www.primarymovement.org

♦ Scotopic Sensitivity Syndrome. Irlen lenses (tinted glasses) have been developed for people with light sensitivity to reduce or eliminate glare which causes some readers to experience visual perceptual difficulties.

♦ Nutrition. There is a theory that a metabolic problem associated with essential fatty acid deficiencies plays a role in the origin of specific learning difficulties

OTHER SPECIFIC LEARNING DIFFICULTIES

The term dyslexia is often written as being synonymous with the terms specific learning difficulties/specific learning disability. This can be very confusing. The term specific learning disability includes dyslexia as one of a number of specific, as distinct from general learning disabilities. Dyslexia is specific to certain aspects of learning. Very often the person with reading difficulty scores in the average or above-average ranges on an intelligence test. The difficulties are not the result of overall or learning disability. Psychologists in reports often describe a child as having a specific learning difficulty of a dyslexic nature.

Since the mid-1990s the term specific learning disability has been used to include dyslexia, dyspraxia, specific language impairment (SLI), attention deficit disorder (ADD)/attention deficit hyperactivity disorder (ADHD) and autistic spectrum disorder. Of these disabilities dyslexia is probably the most recognised. Unfortunately children with dyslexia may also have one or more of the other specific learning disabilities. Research indicates that between 40 and 45 per cent of children with dyspraxia also have dyslexia, and that around 50 per cent of children with dyslexia also have ADHD. There is also evidence of an overlap between dyslexia and language impairment. Detailed information about these specific learning difficulties with regard to assessment and support can best be obtained from the relevant organisations:

♦ The Dyspraxia Association, 69a Main Street, Leixlip, Co. Kildare. Ph. 01 2957125. www.dyspraxiaireland.com

♦ HADD (for Attention Deficit Disorders), Carmichael House, North Brunswick Street, Dublin 7. Ph. 01 8748349 (Wednesday/Friday mornings). www.carmichaelcentre.ie/hadd.

♦ Aspire (for Autistic Spectrum Disorders), Main Office, Coleraine House, Coleraine St. Dublin 7. Phone 8780027. www.aspire-irl.org

Provision for Students with Dyslexia

3

I became interested in the provision of services for students with dyslexia around 1988 when the twins were assessed for the first time. The lack of services for students with dyslexia at all levels of education was very apparent. Very little progress was made for a very long time. Key difficulties included: a lack of teacher training both pre-service and in-career, a scarcity of educational psychologists and poor levels of identification and assessment of children with dyslexia. The Dyslexia Association of Ireland campaigned vigorously over these years with little success. However since 1998 there have been many welcome developments which include:

- The Education Act 1998.
- The Equal Status Act 2000.
- The Report of the Task Force on Dyslexia.
- The Education (Welfare) Act 2000.
- The Education of Persons with Special Educational Needs Act 2004.
- Establishment of the National Educational Psychological Service (NEPS).
- Establishment of the Special Education Support Service (SESS).
- Increased expenditure on special needs, with increased numbers of special needs teachers.
- Changes in NUI entry requirements.

Supports for students can be classified under legislation, agencies, publications, additional teaching support and other supports such as exemptions from Irish, accommodations in examinations and grants for equipment. ⚡

LEGISLATION
The Education Act 1998

Among the provisions of this Act are the following:

- ◆ The school shall provide education for students which is appropriate to their abilities and needs.

- ◆ The school shall use its available resources to ensure the educational needs of all students, including those with a disability or other special educational need, are identified and provided for.

- ◆ The Board of Management of the school shall publish ... the policy of the school concerning admission to and participation in the school including the policy of the school relating to ... admission to and participation by students with disabilities or who have other special educational needs and ensure that, as regards that policy, principles of equality and the right of parents to send their children to a school of the parents' choice are respected.

- ◆ The Board of Management shall make arrangements for the preparation of a school plan. This plan shall state the objectives of the school relating to equality of access to and participation in the school and the measures the school proposes to take to achieve those objectives including equality of access and participation in the school by students with disabilities or who have other special educational needs.

A grievance procedure is set out in the Act. It provides that the parent of a student or, in the case of a student who is 18, the student may appeal against the decision of a teacher or other member of staff of a school. It also provides an appeal procedure when a student is permanently excluded from school or a school refuses to enrol a student. The parents have the right to appeal to the Secretary General of the Department of Education and Science after they have been informed of the decisions by the school and have gone through any appeals procedure offered by the school.

The Education (Welfare) Act 2000

This Act safeguards every child's entitlement to an appropriate minimum education. It focuses particularly on causes of absenteeism. Included in its provisions are:

♦ The establishment of the National Educational Welfare Board, which has the lead role in implementing the Act. The Board deploys Educational Welfare Officers at local level who promote regular school attendance and prevent absenteeism and early school leaving. These officers focus in particular on children at risk who are experiencing difficulties in school with the purpose of resolving impediments to their regular attendance. Alternative schooling is sought for students who have been expelled, suspended or refused admittance to a school.

♦ School managers have the responsibility of adopting a pro-active approach to school attendance by maintaining a register of students and notifying the Educational Welfare Officer of particular problems in relation to attendance. They should also prepare and implement a school attendance strategy to encourage regular school attendance.

♦ The Act makes specific provision for the continuing education and training of young persons aged sixteen and seventeen years who leave school early to take up employment.

♦ The central role of parents in providing for their child's education is recognised. Parents should send their children to school on each school day or otherwise ensure they are receiving an appropriate minimum education. If the child is absent, the parents should notify the principal of the school of the reason for the absence.

The Education of Persons with Special Educational Needs Act 2004

This Act provides for the inclusive education for the child with special educational needs (SEN) in mainstream schooling. It defines a child with SEN as one who learns differently. This definition positively includes children with dyslexia. The Act set up the National Council for Special Education. Among the duties of the Council are the following:

- ◆ To communicate to schools and parents information on best practice concerning the education of children with SEN.
- ◆ To plan and co-ordinate provision for the education and support services for children with SEN.
- ◆ To assess and review resources required for the educational provision for children with SEN.

The Council employs Special Educational Needs Organisers (SENOs) who give advice and assistance to schools. They have a role in planning an individual education plan (IEP) for the student with SEN in collaboration with the teachers and parents of the child. They decide on applications from schools for extra resources for students with SEN such as additional teaching, transport, equipment or the provision of a special needs assistant.

The Act sets out that if the principal of a school is of the opinion that a student is not benefiting from educational programme provided in the school and that these difficulties arise from a special educational need, that the principal, in consultation with the parents, shall arrange for an assessment of the student as soon as possible and not later than one month.

If the assessment establishes that the student has special educational needs, the principal, within one month of receipt of the assessment, will ensure an education plan for the student is drawn up. The contents of such a plan are specified in the Act. The principal should give parents and the SENO a copy of the plan.

The Council has the power to designate the school which a child with SEN is to attend and that school shall admit the child on being so directed by the Council. The Council has to take into account in making such a designation the needs of the child, the wishes of the child's parents and the capacity of the school to accommodate the child and to meet his/her needs.

The Act contains an appeals procedure for parents if they believe the special educational needs of their child are not being addressed.

Equal Status Act 2000

This Act prohibits discrimination on nine separate grounds such as race and religion. One of these grounds is disability. The Act states that educational establishments shall not discriminate in relation to the admission of a student or access or participation of a student on any course.

AGENCIES
National Educational Psychological Service (NEPS)

The National Educational Psychological Service was established in 1999 and is an executive agency of the Department of Education and Science. The development plan for NEPS provides for the gradual expansion over a period of years, with the number of psychologists increasing to two hundred.

NEPS has been delegated authority to develop and provide an educational psychological service to all students in primary and post-primary schools and in certain other centres supported by the Department. NEPS provides the following services to schools:

♦ Consultation and casework about individual students.

♦ Work of a more preventive or developmental nature.

Each psychologist is responsible for a number of schools. The school authorities provide names of children who are giving cause for concern and discuss the relative urgency of each case during the psychologist's visit. This allows the psychologist to give priority to urgent cases. Where cases are less urgent, the psychologist, as a preliminary measure, acts as a consultant to teachers and parents, and offers advice about educational/behavioural plans and monitors progress. The psychologist is also involved in assessing students for reasonable accommodation in state examinations.

Until NEPS becomes fully staffed, there will be a backlog of assessments. Priority is given to those students in greatest need. As a result there may be waiting lists. Consequently many parents opt for private assessments. Tax relief was introduced on the fees paid on private assessments. This is claimed by using the MED 1 form. The NEPS website is found on the Department of Education and Science website www.education.ie.

Special Education Support Service (SESS)

This service was set up in 2003. The aim of the service is to enhance the quality of teaching and learning with particular reference to the education of children with special needs. It is targeted at teachers in mainstream primary and post-primary schools as well as special schools.

SESS provides this service through the following initiatives:

♦ It provides teachers with professional development. An example of such support is subsidising the cost of on-line training courses offered by the Institute of Child Education and Psychology Europe on topics such as dyslexia, ADHD, autism and inclusion.

♦ The provision of in-service training on special education topics.

♦ Telephone and on-line query service.

♦ Local Initiative Schemes, where schools can apply for assistance to meet their needs on special education. This assistance may be financial, professional or advisory.

The SESS website is www.sess.ie. It is a comprehensive website offering information on categories of special needs, resources available, courses available, latest developments in special education and a quick reference to official documents such as Department of Education and Science circulars and legislation on the topic of Special Education.

National Council for Special Education (NCSE)

The National Council for Special Education (www.ncse.ie) was set up under the Education of Persons with Special Education Needs Act 2004. The details of the work of the Council were outlined at the beginning of this chapter in the section on the Education of Persons with Special Educational Needs Act.

PUBLICATIONS

Report of the Task Force on Dyslexia

In 2000 a Task Force on Dyslexia was set up whose brief was to examine the current range of educational provision and support services available to children with specific reading disabilities in Ireland, to assess the adequacy of current educational provision and support services and to make recommendations for the development of policy approaches, educational provision and support services.

The report was completed in 2001 and published on the Government website at www.education.ie. The Task Force looked for submissions from the public and received 399 written submissions. The Task Force also decided to look for oral submissions from the public. This recognised the fact that some individuals with dyslexia would find it easier to make an oral submission than a written one. Adverts quoting a free telephone number were made on the radio. As a result 896 oral submissions were received.

The Task Force gave a definition of dyslexia which recognised the broad range of difficulties which arise from the condition and which also took into account recent research findings. (See Chapter 2). It is a common misperception of dyslexia that it has to do only with reading and spelling and so this definition is very useful as it acknowledges the wide range of difficulties that may be present.

A welcome statement in the report is that "*each student with learning difficulties arising from dyslexia should receive a level of provision appropriate to his/her needs*". The Task Force recommended that since the difficulties presented by students with dyslexia range along a continuum from mild to severe, *there is a need for a continuum of interventions and other services*.

The Task Force suggested a scheme that would involve class teacher, learning support teacher and parents working in co-operation to support the child. The role and contribution of parents is emphasised throughout the report.

It is well worthwhile for parents and teachers to read the full report. There is an executive summary and a summary of the recommendations. These tend to be formally expressed and need to be read carefully to understand their implications. However, throughout the report itself, very practical advice is given. It is here that one can see the influence of the contribution made by parents and students themselves. The everyday language used reflects the voices of the contributors. One section lists practices to be avoided by teachers such as

♦ Asking the student to read aloud in class, unless she/he wishes to do so and she/he has practised in advance.

♦ Asking the student to copy large amounts of material from the blackboard.

♦ Asking a student to rewrite work because of spelling errors.

♦ Penalising a student for not completing tasks within strict time limits.

Such sensible and clear suggestions are invaluable when considering how classroom teachers can help students.

The first recommendation of the report was that appropriate printed and electronic material on dyslexia be distributed to all schools. This has resulted in the publication of the video/CD/DVD *Understanding Dyslexia*.

Understanding Dyslexia Video/CD/DVD

This video/CD/DVD is a joint initiative of the Departments of Education in Ireland, North and South, and was issued to all schools in 2005. It includes:

♦ The video which has eight sections and features professionals, parents, students and adults with dyslexia. This is a very good introduction to the topic of dyslexia in Ireland. Topics covered include the signs and facts about dyslexia, recognition of dyslexia, possible interventions and how parents and teachers can help.

♦ The CD ROM is a comprehensive and invaluable resource for teachers and other professionals dealing with dyslexia. The contents are too extensive to list here, but to give some idea the following are included

  ✧ The Task Force Report.

  ✧ A discussion on the definition of dyslexia.

  ✧ Advice and strategies for teachers, both primary and post-primary and for parents. These can be downloaded as booklets.

  ✧ A very useful self-help section for the pupil as well as a form which the student can use to request help from teachers.

  ✧ Comprehensive listing of resources such as books, websites, tests and teaching materials.

♦ The DVD which includes both the video and the information on the CD ROM.

This package is so useful, it should be widely used. Too often packages such as these can lie on shelves in a staff room of the school. Schools should copy it and give it to all the staff in the school and to parents of students with dyslexia.

Inclusion of Students with Special Educational Needs: Post-Primary Guidelines.

These guidelines were published in 2007 and set out advice and a best practice model for school managements and teachers in relation to the education of students with special educational needs. They advocate a whole-school approach to policy development and implementation. Advice is provided on the role of each staff member in the school. Suggestions are made about the means by which existing resources including staff can be organised effectively.

Of particular interest to parents are the following sections:

♦ Section 1 where the historical background to inclusion, the current provision and legislation are outlined.

♦ Pages 33/34 where the rights of parents under the Education of Persons with Special Educational Needs Act are summarised.

♦ Pages 44/45 where school enrolment policy is discussed.

♦ Page 50 where class placement arrangements for students with special educational needs are discussed. Here schools are advised to include all students in mainstream mixed ability class groups to the greatest extent possible.

♦ Section 4 deals with Individual Education Plans.

These guidelines are available from Government Publications Office at a cost of €10.

Guidelines for teachers of students with general learning difficulties

These guidelines, issued in 2007 on a CD, are aimed at teachers of students with mild, moderate and severe learning difficulties at primary level and students of mild learning difficulties at post primary. The guidelines have been circulated to all schools. They identify potential areas of difficulty, their implications for learning and possible teaching strategies. They include suggested methodologies, exemplars of approach and worksheets. At post-primary level, there are comprehensive and very practical sections for teachers of most post-primary subjects including Art, Business Studies, CSPE, Drama, English, Gaeilge, Geography, History, Home Economics, Music, Physical Education, Religion, Science, SPHE and Technology.

Learning Support Guidelines

The Learning Support Guidelines were published by the Department of Education and Science in 2000. The primary purpose of these guidelines is to provide practical guidance to teachers and parents on the provision of effective learning support to pupils with low achievement/learning difficulties. The guidelines address the following topics:

- ♦ The principles of good practice in the provision of learning support in schools.
- ♦ The need for a policy statement on the provision of learning support in the context of a whole-school plan.
- ♦ The adoption of a collaborative approach by those involved including the principal teacher, class teachers, the learning support teacher and the parents.
- ♦ Screening and identification of pupils, selection of pupils for supplementary teaching and evaluation of the progress of the pupil at the end of each term.
- ♦ Details of the individual profile and learning programme which should be drawn up for each pupil receiving additional help.

Additional Teaching Support

The Department of Education and Science provides additional teaching support for students with dyslexia in three different ways.

- ♦ Extra teaching support through the provision of learning support or resource teaching.
- ♦ Special classes attached to a mainstream school.
- ♦ Special schools for children with specific learning difficulties.

This support is targeted at those students in greatest need as defined by the Department of Education and Science criteria. As a result not all students with dyslexia qualify for such support. The Report of the Task Force on Dyslexia described dyslexia as occurring in a continuum from mild to severe. It recommended the adoption of a model of provision based on meeting the needs for each student. A continuum of interventions should be available to students matched to the severity and persistence of their learning difficulties.

Extra Teaching Support

The terms resource, learning support and remedial have been used to describe additional teaching support provided for children.

Resource teaching is granted based on an individual application for a child with special educational needs to the SENO for the school. Such applications have to be accompanied by relevant psycho-educational/medical reports.

Learning support teaching is provided to children with low achievement. It was formerly called remedial teaching. It does not need an individual application. Assessment for access to such help is done in school through the use of standardised testing. The Learning Support Guidelines state that when selecting pupils for such help, priority should be given to those who achieve scores that are at or below the 10th percentile on a standardised test of English or mathematics.

Increasingly the term special needs teacher is being used which may refer to both learning support and resource teaching.

The Department of Education and Science Circulars SP ED 01/05 and SP ED 09/04 set out new arrangements for the allocation of special education resources at primary level. In May 2005 the Minister of Education and Science, Mary Hanafin, announced further changes in the allocation of these resources. A weighted allocation has been introduced to cater for pupils with higher incidence special educational needs and those with learning support needs, i.e. those functioning at or below the 10th percentile on a standardised test of English and/or mathematics. The circular states the higher incidence special educational needs are borderline mild general disability, mild general learning disability and specific learning difficulty.

◆ The weighted system meant that special needs teaching posts are granted on the following basis:

◆ In all-boy schools the first special education teaching post at 135 pupils, a second post at 295, and so on.

◆ In mixed schools, one post for 145 pupils, a second post at 315 pupils and so on.

◆ In all-girl schools the first post at 195 pupils, the second at 395 pupils and so on.

◆ In disadvantaged schools the first post at 80 pupils, the second at 160 pupils and so on.

◆ There was also increased provision made for smaller schools.

There are children in the higher incidence group in the education system at the present time who have been granted individual allocations. These allocations will continue for these students until they leave the school.

In addition there are specific allocations in respect of pupils with low incidence disabilities. The low incidence disabilities include: physical impairment, hearing impairment, visual impairment, emotional disturbance, severe emotional disturbance, autism, autistic spectrum difficulties, moderate general learning disability and specific speech and language disorder. Applications for these pupils are made on an individual basis to the SENO.

At second-level, Circular PPT 01/05 advises school authorities of the establishment of the National Council for Special Education. It also refers to three other circulars: M 08/99, SP ED 07/02, and SP ED 08/02. These circulars form the basis for determining if a child has a special educational need and what extra teaching or other supports should be put in place. Circular SP ED 08/02 states that for students to qualify for resource teaching under the heading specific learning difficulty, they must have been assessed by a psychologist as:

◆ Being of average intelligence or higher.

◆ Having a degree of learning disability specific to the basic skills in reading, writing or mathematics which places them at or below the 2nd percentile on suitable, standardised, norm referenced tests.

Application for resource hours is made in February. Parents of students entering second level should ensure that the school has the necessary psycho-educational assessment reports by this stage if an application for resource teaching is to be made. It means that, in the case of students for whom resource teaching is appropriate, the school can apply to the Special Educational Needs Organiser (SENO) for the necessary resource allocation and have it in place by the September of entry.

The learning support teacher provides learning support to students with low achievement. The *Learning Support Guidelines* set out that supplementary teaching should be provided to students who have not yet achieved basic competence in English and Mathematics i.e. those performing below the 10th percentile on nationally standardised tests of literacy and numeracy.

These criteria for resource and learning support mean that students with dyslexia whose scores are higher than the 2nd or the 10th percentile respectively do not fall within the criteria for additional teaching support.

This is an area of rapid change in education. The Department of Education and Science website www.education.ie, the NCSE website www.ncse.ie and the SESS website www.sess.ie provide access to circulars for those who want to follow the on-going developments in the provision of extra support for students.

Education Plans

Under the Education of Persons with Special Educational Needs Act, an individual education plan (IEP) should be drawn up for the child who has been assessed as having special educational needs. For the child who falls within the criteria for learning support an individual profile and learning programme (IPLP) is drawn up. Both are very similar and record information about learning attainments and learning strengths of the student. Both contain an outline of the learning programme which sets out learning targets and activities. The learning support/resource/special needs teachers have a key role in such planning. However, it is strongly recommended that an inclusive approach involving class teacher(s), parents and students themselves be adopted in both the diagnostic and planning stages and later in implementation and monitoring of such plans.

Special Classes attached to Mainstream Schools

Special classes (units) for children with specific learning difficulties (including those arising from dyslexia) have been established in designated primary schools where there are a sufficient number of students with such difficulties to form a class. The pupil-teacher ratio for these classes is 9:1. Students are placed in the classes for one or two years and then return to mainstream classes.

The criteria for access to such special classes are as follows:

Assessment by a psychologist on a standardised test of intelligence should place general intellectual ability within the average range or above... There must be an obvious discrepancy between general intellectual ability and performance on a standardised test of reading ability... It would be expected that not more than two per cent of the overall student population would be found in this category. Performance in basic literacy skills as measured by a standardised test should be at a very low level compared to the vast majority of students in a similar age cohort. Consideration should also be given to the child's speaking, writing and spelling skills as well as to his/her level of adaptation to learning within mainstream education, to his/her progress in other aspects of the curriculum and to his/her social and personal development... Students transferring to a special school or support unit for students with specific learning difficulties should have completed second class in a primary school or be at least eight years old on the first day of the school year.

Schools for Children with Specific Learning Difficulties.

The Department of Education and Science has established four primary schools for students with specific learning difficulties including those arising from dyslexia. These schools are as follows:

St. Killian's	Bishopstown, Cork.
St. Oliver Plunkett's	Monkstown, Co. Dublin.
Catherine McAuley's	59 Lr. Baggot St., Dublin 2.
St. Rose's	Balrothery, Tallaght, Dublin 24.

The criteria for access to these schools is similar to those for access to special classes.

OTHER SUPPORTS

Exemption from the study of Irish

Irish is a compulsory subject for students in primary and post-primary schools. However students with specific learning difficulties including those arising from dyslexia may be granted an exemption from the study of Irish. Such an exemption is given to students who function intellectually at average or above-average level but have a specific learning difficulty of such a degree of severity that they fail to achieve expected levels of attainment in basic language skills in the mother tongue. The guideline for such exemptions is that the student is achieving at or below the 10th percentile on a standardised norm-referenced test of reading or spelling. Circular M10/94 sets out the details regarding the exemption from Irish. Circulars are on the Department of Education and Science website, www.education.ie and where relevant on the SESS website, www.sess.ie.

The procedure for gaining an exemption involves the parent submitting a written application on behalf of the child to the school principal along with a copy of a report from a psycho-educational assessment that is less than two years old and which recommends that the student should be exempt because the criteria are met. If the school authorities grant an exemption, a certificate is issued and the Department of Education and Science is informed. The exemption granted at primary level will be recognised at second-level and for entry to the National University of Ireland (NUI) colleges. The exemption should be taken into account at entrance assessment when students are transferring to second-level if Irish is included as part of the assessment.

Students who attend the special schools referred to in the previous section of this chapter may apply for an exemption from Irish when leaving these schools.

Exemption from the NUI Third Language Requirement

The National University of Ireland (NUI) comprises the colleges of UCC, UCD, UCG and Maynooth. The entry requirements for NUI colleges specify that a student must pass six subjects in the Leaving Certificate, two at higher level, and that the student must include English, Irish and a third language.

NUI recognises the exemption from Irish granted at primary or post-primary and also allows a student with such an exemption to be exempt from the third language requirement for entry to NUI. This means that students do not have to take Irish and a third language as subjects in the Leaving Certificate. It is important to apply to NUI, preferably during fifth year, for recognition of the Irish exemption and to apply for the third language exemption.

If students are not exempt from Irish, they may still qualify for an exemption from the third language requirement. NUI considers applications for such an exemption from students who are certified by a qualified professional as having a serious dyslexic condition. The application should be made prior to entry to senior cycle at second level, before subject choice for the Leaving Certificate has been made. Forms are available from NUI at 49 Merrion Square, Dublin 2. (See appendix B).

It is vital when applying to the CAO that information about such exemptions is provided and that it is mentioned on the statement of application which each applicant receives in April/May from the CAO.

Reasonable Accommodations in State Examinations

Reasonable accommodation is the phrase used to describe the various types of support provided for students in the state examinations. An explanatory note is placed on the statement of results when a student avails of these accommodations.

The types of help include:

♦ Reading Assistance. A reader should only be granted where a candidate is unable to read the question paper. This means the candidate must have a severe reading difficulty, and that in the absence of the assistance of a reader, the candidate would be unable to take the examination at all. The explanatory note on the certificate and statement of results will read "*all parts of the examination in this subject were examined except the reading element*".

♦ Tape recorder or computer. The use of a tape recorder or computer is appropriate where it can be established that the candidate has good oral ability, good knowledge of the course content, a score well below average on a spelling test and more than twenty per cent of the target words unrecognisable under test and on written samples. The explanatory note on the English result will read *"all parts of the examination in this subject were assessed except spelling and written punctuation elements"*. In the other language subjects it will read *"all parts of the examination in this subject were assessed except for the spelling and some grammatical elements"*.

♦ A waiver from the spelling and grammatical components in language subjects. This waiver is considered appropriate where it can be established that the candidate has good oral ability, good knowledge of the course content, a score well below average on a spelling test and that the target word is easily recognisable as the target word, although mis-spelt. The explanatory note is similar to that for the tape recorder or computer.

♦ Extra time to be given for the examination. An additional twenty minutes is given for each examination session in the subjects Irish, English, History, Economic History and Geography in the Leaving Certificate examination. All students taking the examination can avail of this time. Other than this provision, extra time is not granted to students with dyslexia. As this accommodation is provided to all students, no explanatory note is on the statement of results.

Students, who are given the accommodation of taping, use of reader or use of word processor, take the examinations in a centre by themselves with a supervisor. Students, who have been granted the accommodation of a waiver from spelling and grammar, take the examination in the main examination centre.

Applications for reasonable accommodation are made by the school. The school sends the application form for accommodations at Leaving Certificate level to the Department of Education and Science and includes a psychological report and samples of the student's work. Parents must sign this form. Applications for accommodations in the Leaving Certificate are made in late May for the following year. It is important that the applications are in by the due date. The application is processed through NEPS. The NEPS psychologist comes to the school to interview the student and staff. In some cases additional testing may be carried out. The psychologist decides if the accommodation is granted. If an application is turned down, there is an appeals procedure.

For the Junior Certificate applications are made in October/November prior to the exam. For Junior Certificate students, there is a less rigorous application process. The form is simpler and there is no need for an assessment to accompany the application. Accommodations are usually granted if the school applies for them. Reasonable accommodation in examinations is discussed at greater length in Chapter 8.

Grants for the purchase of equipment

There is a scheme for the purchase of equipment for pupils with a disability. It applies to pupils who have been diagnosed as having serious physical and/or communicative disabilities of a degree which makes ordinary communication through speech and/or writing impossible for them. The purpose of the scheme is to provide the pupils with equipment which is deemed necessary and of direct educational benefit to them. Examples of such equipment include computers, tape-recorders and word processors. The application is made by the school to the SENO and must be accompanied by a comprehensive professional assessment. If parents buy a computer and/or software for the student, the VAT can be claimed back, using Form VAT 61A, from the VAT Repayments Section, Government Buildings, Kilrush Road, Ennis, Co. Clare. Tel. 065-6849000.

Outstanding Concerns 4

While much progress has been made, particularly in recent years, there are still key difficulties facing the student with dyslexia in the education system. These include:

- The reluctance of some second-level schools to provide equality of access to students with Special Educational Needs and/or dyslexia.
- The lack of psycho-educational assessment at primary school.
- The annotation of the Leaving and Junior Certificate results if the student avails of reasonable accommodations.
- Provision of support for students with dyslexia who do not fall within the guidelines for extra teaching support.
- Aspects relating to the exemption from the study of Irish
- Extra tuition as recommended in the psycho-educational assessment is not recognised for tax relief.
- Lack of teacher training.

EQUALITY OF ACCESS TO SCHOOLS

The thrust of much of the recent legislation is that schools have a responsibility to provide for the needs of the child. The Education Act 1998, the Equal Status Act 2000 and the EPSEN Act 2004 set out the requirement for the school to provide equal access and participation for children with special educational needs. However the reality on the ground is different. The Irish Times have published Department of Education and Science figures which show that special needs provision is largely concentrated in non fee-paying schools and in areas of disadvantage. The statistics show a serious disparity between fee-paying and state schools. The majority of fee-paying schools have less than two percentage of the student population with special needs. Some of the state schools have close to thirty per cent. From my own experience and discussions with parents, it appears that restrictive practices on the part of schools have increased in recent years. It is my belief that this is partially due to an unforeseen consequence to the publication of school league tables. These provide a very public, but single faceted, measurement of a school's performance based on the number of students who go on to third level. It is a very crude instrument to compare schools and does not take into account how schools meet the needs of all the students. The Minister of Education, Mary Hanafin, is on record for stating that some schools are cherry-picking the more able and sending children who present more of an educational challenge elsewhere. She has received complaints from schools that they carry an undue burden in relation to special needs.

The Department of Education Document *Inclusion of Students with Special Education Needs, Post-Primary Guidelines* 2007 states:

'There is evidence that some post-primary schools continue to have restrictive enrolment policies that lead to the effectual exclusion of children with special educational needs and those with other learning differences. Policies and practices may also be in operation within a school that hinder the full participation of children with SEN and there may be a failure to make reasonable accommodations for these students. Some parents of children with SEN have experienced difficulty in relation to the enrolment of their child in the school of their choice. In this regard appeals have been taken successfully by parents under Section 29 of the Education Act 1998.

Boards of management should note that discrimination by educational establishments on the ground of disability including the admission or the terms or conditions of admission of a person as a student is prohibited by the Equal Status Act 2000. Boards of management are also required under the Education Act 1998 to make reasonable provision and accommodation for student with a disability or other special education needs. The Department of Education and

Science considers that the practice of selecting certain students for enrolment and refusing others so as to ensure that only a certain cohort of students is enrolled – for example those who are more able academically – is unacceptable and that where such practices exist they should be discontinued. In such cases schools are strongly advised that their enrolment policies should be revised immediately in conformity with current statutory requirements and to provide for clear and inclusive enrolment practices and procedures. The importance of developing appropriate dispositions, attitudes and skills for inclusion among those working in the school and among the student body and the parent community is also emphasised.

It is also inappropriate for a school to include a clause in its admissions policy to the effect that the enrolment of a student with special educational needs is dependent on the allocation of appropriate resources. It is good practice for a school to seek all relevant information on a child with special educational needs before their enrolment. This may be done as part of the admissions process. ... This information should not be normally used in any way, explicitly or implicitly, to determine whether the child is to be enrolled in the school. Access to such information can however enable the school to make suitable advance preparations for the admission of the student and, if necessary, to seek additional resources from the National Council for Special Education, the Department of Education and Science or the Health Service Executive.'

It is against the thrust of all the recent inclusive legislation that schools would try to exclude students who have learning difficulties and yet the schools have arrived with subtle ways of doing just that. Parents have spoken about the fact that some school principals attempt to persuade them that the school would not be suitable for their child with a learning difficulty. They point to a lack of resources and/or experience in teaching students with such difficulties and argue that other schools might have more. They may even mention the *academic* ethos of their own school or point to the fact that all students must study one or even two foreign languages. In some cases such persuasion occurs despite the fact that the student's siblings are already attending the school. It seems to be inequitable that a school is willing to enrol some children in a family but is unwilling to enrol the child with learning difficulties. Reluctance to enrol students with learning difficulties means that up to ten per cent of the population may not be considered appropriate intake. Imagine if this was a physical disability and the schools could argue that a child with glasses or a limp could not be catered for adequately and that the appropriate placement was in other schools.

The reality is that under the Education Act all schools should provide equality of access and appropriate educational provision to meet the needs of the child. The school cannot discriminate on the grounds of disability. If the school argues that there is a lack of resources or experience, the solution is to ask the NCSE for the resources or SESS to provide in-service training to upgrade the skill level of the teachers. Also it is unfair on schools with inclusive policies if such schools are expected to enrol a disproportionate number of students with learning difficulties. It is easier to adapt teaching strategies and classroom management with a small number of SEN students. Large number of students with SEN in a classroom will affect the teaching and class dynamic. With the media focusing on league tables based on student results, the true achievement of such schools may not be appreciated.

If parents have decided to send their child to a particular school and have concerns about the possible school attitude, one strategy is that they do not tell the school about the needs of the student until they have first been offered a place in the school. At this stage discussions should then be centred on how the school can best meet the needs of the student.

Another strategy for parents, if concerned about the attitude of the school to learning difficulties, is to ask questions from the list below and ask for written answers in reply from the school principal.

♦ Under the Education Act 1998 the Board of Management is required to publish the school policy on pupils with disabilities. Does the school have such a policy?

♦ Under the same Act the School Plan should state the measures the school proposes to take to achieve equality of access and participation for students with disabilities. Does the School Plan contain such measures?

♦ The Act contains a grievance procedure, which provides a mechanism for parents to raise grievances about a lack of support services. How can parents access such a procedure?

♦ Under the Equal Status Act 2000, educational establishments are prohibited from directly or indirectly discriminating in relation to access and participation. What is the school policy on admissions? What criteria are used?

♦ Some schools use the term *academic* in describing themselves. This is to suggest that as the school is an academic one, the parent should look for a different school to meet the child's needs. What does this term academic mean? Is the school catering only for those who will go on to 3rd level? What about students with dyslexia who have poor verbal-linguistic abilities and who may not perform well at second-level due to the dominance of languages and verbally-based subjects and yet have the ability to go on to 3rd level? Does the definition of academic apply to a top grouping in an intelligence test? Does it mean the school excludes children with learning difficulties? All of these contravene the principle of equality of access. If such a term is used, ask the principal for a written definition of the term as understood by that particular school.

♦ Equality of participation means the school should provide the relevant support services to enable a student participate. The Act requires a school to do all that is reasonable to accommodate the needs of a person with a disability, so long as such provision does not go beyond 'nominal cost'. This is not defined in the Act and such a definition may eventually be determined in the courts. Many of the supports that enable a student with dyslexia to participate fully do not require much finance. These supports may include in-career training for teachers, study skills training for students, photocopying notes and provision of information and advice to parents on the topic.

If the student with difficulties is quiet and well-behaved, it is easier to survive in the school system. However some students with dyslexia become frustrated and this may lead to discipline difficulties. There are also students in the educational system with other learning difficulties such as ADD/ADHD who may have behavioural problems. In the past parents were very much alone when coping with such children. Frequently they were asked to remove the child from school. Frequent long suspensions may have been used as a way to persuade a parent to remove a child. The parents could then find that they could not get the child into another school. Some of these children left education for good in their early teens. This had major implications for their future as it affected their education, career prospects and personal confidence. Some had not achieved adequate literacy skills to be able to read and write. The ESRI in its publication 'Issues in the Employment of Early School Leavers' described the employment prospects for such students as 'low pay, low skill, and frequently temporary' and many young people entering the labour market 'do not have the skills or resources to maintain any long-term position in it'. Under the recent legislation schools have a responsibility to students with behavioural difficulties to try to manage and put in place interventions. If a student is asked to leave the school, parents can appeal such a decision.

If the schools now have greatly increased responsibilities towards students with special needs, they also need resources and funding to enable them to do this. Clearly if a child has major behavioural difficulties, it can lead to disruption in the classroom. This is not fair and equitable to the other pupils in the class. Schools need speedy access to extra resources such as classroom assistants, resource teachers and psychological services to provide appropriate resources for such students.

THE LACK OF PSYCHO-EDUCATIONAL ASSESSMENTS AT PRIMARY SCHOOL.

The Department of Education and Science Circulars SP ED 01/05 and SP ED 09/04 set out new arrangements for the allocation of special education resources at primary level. A weighted allocation has been introduced to cater for pupils with higher incidence special educational needs and those with learning support needs, i.e. those functioning at or below the 10th percentile on a standardised test of

English and/or Mathematics. The circular states the higher incidence special educational needs are borderline mild general disability, mild general learning disability and specific learning difficulty/dyslexia.

There is no individual allocation of extra teaching to children with higher incidence special educational needs. It means that the child with dyslexia is covered by the general allocation of extra teaching resources to the school. There has been a very welcome increase in the number of special education teachers in the school system. The student can access this help without a psycho-educational assessment. This new system is designed to put resources permanently in place in schools and therefore facilitate early and flexible intervention. It allows better planning as schools know the resources available. One of the advantages of this model stated in the Department of Education press release is that it will reduce the need for individual applications and therefore the need for assessments to support such applications.

However the lack of psycho-educational assessments has serious consequences. The reason why a child is not learning to read may not be understood. While teachers may have well-founded suspicions that a student may have dyslexia, an assessment is required for a diagnosis to be made. This could result in the child getting extra teaching support but the reasons why such help is required will not be investigated. In order to provide the most effective intervention, it is necessary to understand the causes of the difficulties. A child with mild general learning difficulty requires different teaching strategies to those required by a child with dyslexia. Parents and students need to know if dyslexia is present and the profile of ability of the student in order to make informed educational choices. Assessments are essential when applying for supports such as exemptions from Irish, reasonable accommodation in exams or access to the support services at second-level or third-level. If the child is not assessed while at primary, it is likely to mean that the relevant supports are not put in place at second-level.

This lack of provision for assessments is compounded by the lack of educational psychologists. The National Educational Psychology Service is understaffed and this can mean that even when a student is entitled to an assessment, there are long waiting lists.

The Explanatory Note on the Statement of Results for Students

An explanatory note is placed on the certificates of students who have availed of reasonable accommodations in the Junior and Leaving Certificate.

This explanatory note on the certificate is a cause of concern to the Dyslexia Association of Ireland (DAI) and to parents. Recommendation eighteen of the Report of the Task Force on Dyslexia states:

> 'In light of recent equality legislation, the Department of Education and Science should refer to the Director of Equality and the National Disability Authority the practice of appending explanatory notes on the certificate of candidates with specific learning difficulties, including those arising from dyslexia, who are granted certain accommodations in state examinations'.

The note is a permanent statement on the certificate of the student. For future employers, who may not be familiar with dyslexia and its effects, the wording of the different explanatory notes might imply the student cannot read, spell or use grammar at all. This is more important for the student who opts for employment directly after second-level. There is no such explanatory note on the certificates and degrees issued by third-level colleges and PLC courses. Employers, in all probability, will not ask to see the Junior or Leaving Certificates of applicants with further qualifications.

In 2006 a case was taken by two Leaving Certificate students to the Equality Tribunal. The Tribunal found that the Department of Education and Science had discriminated against the two students by annotating their results. The Department were instructed to issue new certificates without annotation and to pay €6,000 to each student. The Equality Officer judged that the annotation revealed data about the Leaving Certificate holder which they may not have been otherwise obliged to reveal wherever this was not relevant. In such situations the decision to reveal their disability was taken out the hands of the students. While the integrity of the exams is vital and correctly something to be aspired to, the Equality Officer noted that the Department's position is undermined in relation to annotation when marks that are given to those who sit their examination through Irish is considered. Those students are given an extra 10% in some subjects and 5% in others. The Leaving Certificate of these students bears no indication that an adjustment has been made and they are not annotated in any way.

The Department has appealed the decision and the case was heard in July 2007. The result is expected in October 2007. In the meantime, the Department continues to annotate certificates.

SUPPORT FOR STUDENTS WHO DO NOT QUALIFY FOR ADDITIONAL TEACHING

Some students with dyslexia do not meet the criteria set by the Department of Education for access to extra teaching supports such as learning support/resource teaching. However, they may still experience varying degrees of difficulty in school. The Report of the Task Force on Dyslexia recognised that since the difficulties presented by students with dyslexia range along a continuum from mild to severe, there is a need for a continuum of interventions and other services. Some students with mild or moderate dyslexia may need minimal intervention in order to achieve.

Students with above-average ability and dyslexia may be taking several subjects at higher level in the Leaving Certificate. At this level, the effects of dyslexia may be different than those experienced by younger students. The students may need training in study techniques, interpreting of questions, and structuring answers to help them achieve their potential. The Dyslexia Association of Ireland (DAI) workshop classes and exam preparation classes provide an example of the targeted help that can be provided for such students. The students find such help invaluable. These workshops are run throughout the country. Details of the workshops are available on the DAI website www.dyslexia.ie.

If the student does not fall within the learning support/resource remit, whose responsibility is it to ensure that the recommended continuum of interventions is in place? Whole-school planning should clearly set out the roles and responsibilities of the staff involved.

The Report of the Task Force stressed the key role of the class/subject teacher in providing support. Even if students are receiving learning support/resource teaching, they spend the vast majority of the school day with the mainstream teacher. The student, who receives no additional teaching, relies totally on the class/subject teacher. For this reason it is vital that all teachers receive pre-service and in-career training on the topic of dyslexia. SESS has begun to provide training on the topic of dyslexia at primary and post-primary schools.

IRISH EXEMPTION DIFFICULTIES

The Department of Education and Science had provided the facility that a student may be exempt from the study of Irish. The grounds for such exemptions are set out in Circular M10/94. School managements are authorised to grant exemptions under the rule according with the prescribed procedures and criteria. There are some areas of difficulty with the exemptions:

♦ Parents find it difficult to get information about the exemption and clear guidelines on how it operates. Schools appear not be informed or reluctant to process the exemption. In some cases parents have been persuaded to delay applying for it or have been given information that the child will have to study Irish at second-level so they should continue to study Irish. These comments are based on many, many parents I have spoken to at DAI courses over the last two decades. The Circular states that the assessment must be less than two years old. If this window of opportunity provided by the assessment is not availed of within these two years, a new assessment is needed.

♦ Sometimes, the primary school allows the child not to study Irish and gives extra English, without processing an exemption. The child transfers to second-level without having studied Irish. There is no exemption in place and therefore the child has to study Irish at this stage. The assessment may be out of date, or in the case of a new assessment, the child may have moved above the 10th percentile of achievement in language skills and so does not qualify now for the exemption.

♦ There are many students with dyslexia who find the study of Irish onerous and would benefit from an exemption but who do not fall below the 10th percentile. The Leaving Certificate is a very competitive gateway examination to careers and opportunities. It should be the case that students can present their strongest subjects to compete on an equal footing. Because the Leaving Certificate is such an important examination, it could be argued that Irish should be an optional subject after Junior Certificate for those students who have a diagnosed learning difficulty.

LACK OF TAX RELIEF ON THE COSTS OF EXTRA TUITION

For several years prior to 2006 parents had been able to include fees for DAI workshop tuition when submitting their MED 1 Form to Revenue at the end of the tax year. This form allows taxpayers to claim certain medical expenses against tax. In 2006 the Revenue Commissioners stated that there is no provision in tax law for granting tax relief for tuition for children with dyslexia. The only allowable expenses were for psycho-educational assessments and for speech and language therapy. DAI argues that since the assessment is an allowable expense, the recommendation of the psychologist for extra tuition should be an allowable expense. The Association also argues that speech and language therapy is for children with a spoken language difficulty while workshop tuition is for children with a written language difficulty. The decision of the Revenue Commissioners was reiterated by the Minister of Finance, Mr Cowen, in 2007, in a letter to the DAI. It stated: 'There are no plans to broaden out health expenses relief to include tuition expenses for children with dyslexia.' The DAI had contacted every TD in the country and their case was acknowledged as very reasonable by many of the Dail deputies. DAI continues to lobby to have such relief given and would ask parents to do the same.

LACK OF TEACHER TRAINING

The Task Force on Dyslexia recognised the key involvement of mainstream teachers both in identifying possible learning difficulties arising from dyslexia and in addressing the needs of students identified as having such difficulties. It states that mainstream teachers should assume major responsibility for the progress and development of each student in their classes who has learning difficulties arising from dyslexia, with learning support and resource teachers and other professionals assuming supporting roles. The Task Force recommended that subject teachers "provide differentiated instruction" to such students.

However the reality on the ground is that there is a large number of teachers within the system at second-level who have received no pre-career or in-career training on the topics of special education, dyslexia or differentiated instruction. So students with dyslexia may be in a class with a teacher who does not understand dyslexia and does not have the skills and teaching strategies to make the subject accessible. In a DAI survey in 2006 89% of the parents who replied had experienced difficulty with the level of teacher awareness of dyslexia. The Special Education Support Service has begun to address this lack of training and has started to provide courses for schools.

Choosing a Second-Level School

5

Deciding which second-level school would be the most suitable for a student with dyslexia is a key decision for parents. Some parents may not have a choice since there may be only one school for the area. Other parents have a choice, particularly in city areas.

To make the best choice, the parents of a student with dyslexia need to have as much information as possible about the schools and what they offer. Below are some points to consider when choosing a school. Some of this information will be freely available in school literature. The website www.scoilnet.ie gives access to the websites of schools, as well as information on courses and tips for parents. Some information may be available on request from the school. Parents of students already in the school can also be a source of information.

CLASS PLACEMENT

How does the school place students in classes? Most schools have more than one class in each year group. Different ways to place students in classes include:

1. Mixed ability: The class is made up of students from all ability levels. If a school is taking in one hundred and twenty students, the students are randomly broken into four different groups of thirty. Mixed ability classes are usually arranged for first year only or in some subjects only or until the completion of Junior Certificate. As students progress they are placed in class subject groups according to the programme they are studying for the Certificate examinations.

2. Setting: This means that instead of an overall assessment incoming students are assessed in an individual subject, e.g.

Irish, English or Maths. The students are placed in class on their ability in that subject. A student could be in the top Maths class but in a middle English class. This type of placement takes a lot of school resources because all the classes in a particular subject must be held at the same time. If there are one hundred and twenty students in a year group, a school will need four Maths teachers available at the same time.

3. Streaming: This is where students are placed in classes by their performance at assessment. In the case of one hundred and twenty students, the first thirty could be in the highest stream, the next thirty in the second stream and so on. The class is together for core subjects, typically Irish, English, Maths, Religion, History and Geography.

4. Banding: This is an attempt to merge mixed ability and strict streaming. With 120 students, the top sixty students on assessment would be grouped into one band. Two classes would be formed from this group randomly. The weaker sixty students on assessment would be the second band and again two classes would be formed. It means there is no bottom class.

The Post Primary Guidelines on Inclusion of Students with Special Educational Needs (2007) discusses class place in some detail. It states:

'In general, schools are advised to include all students in mainstream mixed ability class groups to the greatest extent possible and in a manner that allows them to participate in a meaningful and beneficial way in classroom activity. A positive feature of placing students with special educational needs in mixed ability classes is the opportunity they get to learn alongside their typically developing peers. Teachers often state in reports of research into mixed ability teaching that there are beneficial effects to both high-achieving and low-achieving students from placement in mixed ability classes. The benefits include not only academic progress but also social and personal development. Recent research from the ESRI shows an increase in the use of mixed ability classes since the 1990's. The report notes that 70% of schools surveyed used mixed ability in first year, 16% used banding and 14% used streaming. The report concluded that mixed ability grouping is desirable as steaming leads to lower achievement among those in bottom streams and increased transition difficulties for those in higher streams because of academic pressure. Successful learning for students in mixed ability classes depends on such factors as teacher expertise and the conditions for learning, including the implementation of differentiated approaches for teaching and learning, appropriate class size, the availability within the classroom of sufficient space for group activities and suitable resources for learning'.

On the use of steaming or banding, the Guidelines state:

'Advocates of streaming often suggest that the streaming of students in accordance with ability or attainment is not only organisationally attractive but also enables the teachers to concentrate on the priority learning needs of students with low achievement or those with special educational difficulties. ... It is argued that a streamed class group provides a suitable setting in which students with low achievement or with special educational needs can be given the individualised attention they need and the opportunity to make progress at their own rate. However, recent research suggests that the outcomes for students in classes that are streamed in accordance with attainment or ability fall far below these expectations. The negative effects of streaming include the possibility that students may be segregated from their peers rather than included with them. Those in low streams may make poor academic progress and may feel marginalised and isolated within the school community. ... The use of standardised test results as the sole or main criterion for separating students into class groups either before or immediately following entry to the school displays a narrow view and is contrary to best practice'.

Moving Up (2004), a study carried out for the NCCA found that where streaming is used is tends to result in labelling of students as either 'smart' or 'stupid'.

Class placement for the student with dyslexia

A mixed ability system favours students with dyslexia. They are in a class where they will benefit from the wide range of ideas and discussions. They may be able to use their strong abilities in the class room, for example, in debate or class discussion, while at the same time the teacher knows of their weaker literacy skills.

Setting can be of benefit for students with dyslexia as it can take into account their strengths. However, if they are placed in a weak English class because of weaker writing skills, although these skills may benefit from the slower pace set by teachers, they may miss the stimulation and ideas that would be present in a mixed ability class.

Streaming is the most inappropriate method of placement. Students may end up in a lower stream for many reasons. Family problems, lack of support at home for schooling or disruptive behaviour can contribute to poor academic achievement. These problems may spill over into class interactions. The Guidelines indicate the disadvantages of streaming for all students in bottom classes. This is probably the worst scenario for students with dyslexia. The entrance assessment is not likely to show their strengths and unless the psychological assessment is taken into account, they can be placed in a class that will focus on basic skills but will not provide the challenge and stimulus they need and the verbal discussion of which they are capable. They may become bored at the slow pace of the class. In some cases this may result in discipline problems. In a bottom stream class there may be more disaffected and unmotivated students. This can mean that class control can take a larger proportion of the teacher's time with a consequential loss of actual teaching. Students with dyslexia may rely on listening to learn rather than reading, and so constant interruptions can interfere with learning.

There is one very important point about streaming to consider particularly in relation to a student with dyslexia. Take a student who has very weak verbal skills and very good Maths. If the student is placed in a lower stream on account on the poor verbal skills, will it deprive the student of sitting higher level Maths in the Junior Certificate? In some schools this can happen. The student may be placed in a lower stream class and as a consequence will sit ordinary or foundation level Irish, English and Maths in state examinations. If parents are aware that the student has an ability profile with strong Maths, they should check this point at the time the student enters second-level. It is too late to discover the student is taking ordinary level Maths at the end of first year or during second year. The student, by then, will have fallen behind the pace of a higher level Maths class.

Parents should also be aware of the format of the entrance assessment. A reading test will give an indication of the student's ability to read, a spelling test will give an indication of the ability to spell but a Maths test, where the questions are verbally put, may be more a test of the student's ability to understand English rather than Maths and may not give an accurate indication of the student's skills in Maths.

Subject Choice

Parents of a student with dyslexia face the major decision of subject choice when the student begins second-level. This decision can be far more important for students with learning difficulties than for other students as there may be subjects in which these students will not succeed no matter how hard they try and other subjects in which they can make good progress.

Some schools offer a wide choice of Junior and Leaving Certificate subjects while in other schools the choice is more restricted. The subjects on offer depend on the school's resources and the number of pupils attending the school.

A small number of schools have the structure that in the course of first year the student has classes in all the subjects on offer and the decision about subject choice is made at the end of that year. This allows a more informed decision to be made as the student knows the progress made in each subject. More typically the parents and student have to choose subjects when the student is entering second-level.

Students following the Junior Certificate programme in a secondary school must take Irish, English, Maths, History, Geography, CSPE (Civic, Social and Political Education) and SPHE (Social, Personal and Health Education). Religion may or may not be an examination subject. Normally they choose three or four additional subjects called options. The most commonly available options are Art, Business Studies, Home Economics, Languages, Metalwork, Materials Technology, Science or Technical Graphics. There are other subjects in the Junior Certificate examination which a small number of pupils may take such as Technology, Music, Classical Studies, Environmental/Social Studies and Typewriting.

In some option subjects there can be a limit on the number of places due to teacher availability or a maximum class size restriction. The school should have a system for allocating places to such classes.

For some students with dyslexia option choice may be critical. There may be some subjects they will enjoy and do well in and other subjects in which they will find it difficult to make progress whereas a student not affected by dyslexia may achieve equally well in all subjects. When students have a number of subjects they enjoy, it can change the whole attitude to school. Parents should ask well in advance how places in option classes are allocated so that they can obtain the most appropriate options. In some cases, because of the importance of the student taking the most appropriate subjects, a case for positive discrimination in allocating option places could be made. It would be helpful if such a suggestion was contained in the student's psycho-educational assessment report.

Most students will take nine or ten subjects in the Junior Certificate. For some students severely affected with dyslexia, this may be a particularly heavy burden. The option structure may provide a way to reduce the number of subjects being taken. This is how it could work. The student will take the core subjects, English, Maths, History, CSPE, SPHE, Geography and Irish (unless the student is exempt from Irish). The possible option structure offered by a school might be that the students take one subject from each of the following lines, giving them four option subjects.

1. French, Art, Business Studies.
2. Science, Business Studies, Home Economics, German.
3. Science, Materials Technology, Technical Graphics, Business Studies.
4. Art, Science, Home Economics.

A student could take the same subject, such as Science, from two different lines. This would reduce the number of subjects studied for the Junior Certificate and double the amount of teaching received in that subject. This is an extreme solution. Most students with dyslexia are well able to cope taking all the option subjects and, in my experience, have actually enjoyed their option subjects more than their core subjects. However such a reduction of options may be helpful in the case of students who are severely affected by dyslexia and are struggling to achieve literacy.

It is difficult to give general advice on which subjects would suit a student with dyslexia as each student has a different profile of abilities. Here is information about subjects which may help in reaching a decision.

Art

Art is a subject without a written exam at Junior Certificate level. At Leaving Certificate level the paper includes written questions on the History of Art. 75% of the final grade in the Junior Certificate is based on projects which the student completes during the exam year. Because the subject is not verbally based, it can provide a rewarding and stimulating subject to students with dyslexia, many of whom have good visual spatial skills. Indicators for success in the subject would be an interest in art and crafts and good hand-eye co-ordination.

Business Studies

Business Studies is one subject at Junior Certificate and splits into the three separate subjects of Accounting, Economics and Business at Leaving Certificate. It contributes to the student's understanding of the world of business and encourages a positive attitude to enterprise. The course includes both book-keeping and theoretical content. The book-keeping aspect of the course may be attractive to the students with dyslexia who have good computational skills. It would be recommended that the student who intends to take Accountancy at Leaving Certificate level should take Business Studies at Junior Certificate level. It is easier to take up Business and Economics at Leaving Certificate as new subjects.

Home Economics

Home Economics is a subject with a mixture of practical skills and theoretical content. There is a project and a practical cookery examination during the Junior Certificate year, both of which carry marks towards the Junior Certificate exam. It leads on to the subjects of Home Economics Social and Scientific and Home Economics

General at Leaving Certificate. Career possibilities include hotel and catering, food science, fashion, interior design and paramedical careers. Indicators for success in this subject are an interest in the subject matter and good dexterity.

Languages

Should the student with dyslexia take a foreign language? This is a key question for parents. The importance of languages is being stressed as Ireland trades increasingly with EU partners. Also it is widely believed that students need a third language as an entry requirement for university. This third language requirement applies only to the colleges of NUI. Students with serious dyslexia can apply for an exemption from this requirement. See Appendix B.

Some students with dyslexia will never make a success of studying a language and it will become a subject in which they face constant failure. This can have an effect on how they view school. Indicators that the student should not take a foreign language include difficulty in reading and spelling in English, poor achievement in Irish, difficulties remembering the sound of new words and recall of new vocabulary. However the language courses have an increasing oral and aural element, so students with good oral and aural ability may be quite successful in mastering another language. Some schools have an option structure that makes the study of a foreign language obligatory and this may not suit particular students with dyslexia. This is a school-based decision to make the study of a foreign language mandatory. It is not a regulation of the Department of Education and Science.

Materials Technology (wood)

Materials Technology (wood) consists of practical work, theory and drawing. It aims to train students in the use of tools and materials and to develop self-reliance, initiative and accuracy. The Junior Certificate exam consists of a written theory examination and a practical project. It is studied at Leaving Certificate level as Construction Studies and is suited to those interested in careers in construction, architecture and engineering. Indicators for success in the subject are: dexterity, an interest in the subject and a practical approach to problem solving.

Metalwork

Metalwork introduces students to the various processes, tools and materials in modern use. It has a practical and theoretical content. The student can gain experience in interpreting drawings, planning a work sequence and carrying out a task. At Leaving Certificate the subject is studied as Engineering and provides a sound and knowledgeable basic grounding for those interested in engineering or technical careers. Indicators for success in the subject are: dexterity, an interest in how things work and a logical approach to problem solving.

Science

Science is taught as one subject at Junior Certificate level but splits into the three separate subjects of Physics, Chemistry and Biology at Leaving Certificate level. It opens the doors to careers in technology, medicine and science. A science subject is a minimum requirement for entry to many third-level courses in these areas. The answers required in the Junior Certificate are factually based with very little essay type answers. This may suit the student with dyslexia. The course includes a large amount of practical laboratory work. Because of the need to be scientifically literate in the modern world, it is advisable for most students to take Science as a subject.

Technical Graphics

In Technical Graphics students are trained in the use of drawing instruments and are given a knowledge of the basic geometrical constructions and their practical applications. This subject leads to the study of Technical Drawing at Leaving Certificate and is suited to those interested in careers in architecture, engineering and other occupations of a technical nature. Indicators for success in the subject are: neatness, good hand-eye co-ordination and a logical approach to problems. Some students with dyslexia excel in visual spatial skills and this subject will suit such students.

The subjects Art, Home Economics, Materials Technology, Business Studies (book-keeping element), Metalwork, Science and Technical Graphics have a practical and theoretical content. As a result the student is learning through doing tasks and developing skills as well as learning the theory content. The skills developed are then tested in the exam. This can mean there is less memorising of large amounts of facts. This reduction in rote memory work as well as the multi-sensory approach can suit the student with dyslexia.

One subject that a small number of students take is Typewriting. It is a skills-based subject. Students with dyslexia should develop keyboard skills as soon as possible. Typewriting provides a subject in which they might be successful and which would equip them with these essential skills.

One aspect of the Junior Certificate and Leaving Certificate courses is the increase in projects and practicals which are now included as part of the examination. At Junior Certificate level, students may have some form of assessment during the course of the year in the subjects, Religion, Science, Home Economics, Art, Metalwork, Materials Technology and CSPE. Many of these occur in the period March/April. Many students procrastinate and leave things to the last minute. This approach does not suit many students with dyslexia who may be overwhelmed by the different demands of the projects and course work. Parents can be of help here by making sure they inform themselves of the project deadlines and then by helping the student to schedule the work over several weeks.

IRISH

The student may be exempt from Irish under the Department of Education and Science Directive. Rule 46 of the Rules and Programme for Secondary Schools allows some students with dyslexia an exemption from Irish. One of the grounds for such an exemption is that it is given to students who function intellectually at average or above average level but have a specific learning difficulty of such a degree of severity that they fail to achieve expected levels of attainment in basic language skills in the mother tongue. The guideline is that the student is in the bottom 10% of achievement on a standardised norm-referenced test of reading or spelling. School authorities must receive a psycho-educational assessment that is less than two years old, and must issue a certificate to the student and forward a copy to the Department of Education and Science. Students who attend the special reading schools such as Catherine

McAuley's School in Baggot St. and St. Oliver Plunkett's School in Monkstown may apply for an exemption when leaving these schools.

Some students may fall within this guideline at one stage, but with additional tuition, may develop their skills in English. Therefore at one stage they might qualify for such an exemption and, if tested at a later stage, might not.

If the student qualifies for the exemption at a particular point in time, it would be prudent to actually get the official letter showing this exemption. Parents may decide to let a student, who is exempt, participate in Irish class in order to benefit from the cultural aspects of the subject. They will then have the option further on in the education system to withdraw the student from Irish because they have the exemption in writing. This could be of major benefit to senior-cycle students who intend to apply to the Central Applications Office (CAO). Entry to CAO colleges is determined by points. Senior-cycle students should be able to present their best subjects for examination to maximise points and be able to compete on level terms.

Take the case of a student in 2004, with very good Maths and technical ability but poorer verbal abilities, who applied for an Engineering degree in one of the National University of Ireland (NUI) colleges. The entry requirements for NUI colleges state that students must have English, Irish and a third language. This student began his Leaving Certificate course taking nine subjects. He did not qualify for an Irish exemption as he was outside the 10th percentile. He was studying English, Irish and French at ordinary level due to weaker verbal skills. He then had to take six other subjects at higher level in order to maximise his points. His higher level subjects were Maths, Applied Maths, Physics, Geography, Technical Graphics and Accounting. Most Leaving Certificate students do seven subjects. This student, who has a learning difficulty, was in the position of having to take two additional subjects outside school time. With his language difficulties, the study of Irish was very demanding and it took more effort to get the D grade in ordinary level Irish than to achieve in higher grades in his higher level subjects. He applied for and received an exemption from the NUI third language requirement in the course of fifth year. This reduced the number of his subjects to eight. He achieved 475 points based on his six higher level subjects. He therefore got a place on his chosen course. This student was fortunate in the educational choices made by his family. If he had not had the two additional subjects he would have achieved 365 points, a difference of 110 points.

The exemption from Irish at primary level is recognised at post-primary level. NUI recognises the exemption in respect to its entry requirements and also allows a student with such an exemption to be exempt from the third language requirement for entry to NUI colleges. (See Appendix B).

There are some careers where a certain standard of Irish is required. A 'C' in higher level Irish in the Leaving Certificate is necessary for primary teaching. The Gardai did have a requirement that the student needed a pass in Irish in the Leaving Certificate and that a 'B' grade in foundation was acceptable. This has now been changed to applicants needing two languages (English and another). It affects a small number of career choices if the student does not study Irish.

Sometimes a teacher at primary level, recognising the child's difficulties, allows the child to do extra English work during the allocated time for Irish. However the official exemption has not been issued. If the student is not studying Irish at primary level and meets the criteria for the awarding of an exemption, it is very important for a parent to ask the school to issue the certificate of exemption and notify the Department of Education and Science. Otherwise the child will be required to study Irish when attending second-level.

If the student is exempt from Irish, there should be provision for this class time to be used constructively such as learning support withdrawal, additional English reading or computer time.

Is Irish part of the entrance assessment? If it is, does it play a part in deciding class placement? If the student has an exemption or has attended one of the specialised reading schools, such as St. Oliver Plunkett's in Monkstown where the emphasis is on mastery of English, with less emphasis on Irish, is this taken into account in decisions on class placement?

Learning Irish can cause some students with dyslexia particular difficulties. The phonics are different so the child who relies on phonics to read and spell can have difficulty. This would also apply to other languages. However adding to the difficulties is the fact that in Irish the order of the words in the sentence also changes with the verb coming first. Students with sequencing difficulties can find this difficult. Also the beginning of the word can change with prefixes in certain grammatical constructions, so the word may not be found in the dictionary if the student tries to look it up.

The Task Force on Dyslexia recognised the lack of assessment instruments and support materials for students whose first language and/or main language of instruction is Irish and recommended that the Department of Education and Science should commission the development of such materials.

Discipline

Students with dyslexia tend to be disorganised. They need a clearly organised classroom with clearly given instructions and a sense of order as they may need to concentrate quite hard to interpret their teacher's instructions. Some learn much more from listening attentively than they would from reading from a textbook. They require a well-structured and disciplined atmosphere in which to learn. Such a classroom provides the teacher with time to ensure the student understands what is expected and allows the teacher to check individual work. It also ensures a pleasant and relaxing environment. In a classroom where the teacher has to impose order constantly, the teacher can be more stressed and have less time to give to individual students. The atmosphere is more fraught. The flow of the teacher's input is interrupted because of the need to correct students.

In recent years teachers have observed a greater indiscipline in the classroom. The reasons for this are varied. They include: increased amount of family breakdown, less parenting skills so some parents find it difficult to discipline their children and children with little regard for authority who find it difficult to obey discipline imposed by others. The final sanctions open to schools have been reduced. Expulsion of a pupil is extremely rare. Whatever the reasons, there is no doubt the student's progress will be affected if there is difficulty imposing order on a class group.

Students, who are different in any way, may be picked on by bullies. Students with dyslexia may be considered different and may become victims of such behaviour. Most schools now have strong anti-bullying policies. However school authorities need to be informed if bullying is happening. It is possible to prepare students to meet bullying behaviour by teaching them coping strategies in advance. Giving them an understanding that such behaviour is a reflection of inadequacies on the part of the bully may prevent them feeling that there is something wrong with themselves which attracts bullying. Make sure that, if a situation arises, that they know they should talk to the adults in authority.

The Post Primary Guidelines on the Inclusion of Students with Special Educational Needs 2007 states:

> 'Students with special educational needs may be vulnerable to physical, psychological or emotional harassment. If these students are subjected to unfair treatment within the school by staff members or by students, the physical, psychological and educational effects can be very damaging for them. The failure by a school to take reasonable steps to prevent harassment, including the inclusion of preventive measures in school policies and procedures may result in the school being held liable under the Equal Status Act 2000 ... Each member of the school community has the right to participate, both physically and psychologically in a secure manner and in atmosphere free from discrimination, prejudice harassment or bullying. A person in authority must not harass a student who has applied for admission or who avails of any service in the school'.

TRANSITION YEAR

In some schools transition year is part of the curriculum for all students. In others it is not available and in some it is optional. There can be advantages and disadvantages to a transition year for students with dyslexia.

The advantages of transition year include:

♦ The student with dyslexia may find it difficult to achieve academically. Transition year gives the opportunity to do projects, to obtain new skills, to research possible careers and to experience different methods of working. It is different from the academic work done for the Junior Certificate and the student may do well with this change of approach. Self-esteem may be fragile in the student, who may have had to come to terms with failure in academic areas in the past. Transition year may give the opportunity to build up self-esteem. Up to now the class may have judged and assessed fellow-students on academic results. This year will allow other aspects of the personality to show.

♦ It gives time to reflect on the type of CV the student has and how to develop it. Some students will not achieve the academic results to compete for courses where points decide the allocation of places. They may be relying on a good CV to help them at interviews.

♦ Project work will help the student to organise goals, to do research and to meet deadlines. These are skills which many students with dyslexia need to develop. However they may need help and support to do it.

♦ Self-esteem can be enhanced during transition year by

  ✧ Work experience.

  ✧ Learning new skills, such as computer skills, typing and organising projects. If the student does not already use a computer, it is important to become skilled with computers during this year.

  ✧ Contributing to the community. This can be the school community or the wider community. Many transition year programmes include a community element, e.g. fund-raising for charities.

  ✧ Achievements such as the President's Award Scheme (An Gaisce), or sporting exploits all build up self-esteem. The President's Award is particularly suitable as the student chooses four challenges in each of the following; community work, sport, new skills and an adventurous activity. If students meet their goals, the award is given.

The disadvantages of a transition year for the student include:

♦ The programme for transition year may lack structure in some schools and students may lose the study skills they have learned and find it hard to return to serious study in fifth year.

♦ The students with dyslexia may already be older than classmates if there has been a repeat year at some stage. Taking transition year may mean they are relatively old sitting the Leaving Certificate.

♦ These students may feel somewhat at sea in the unstructured curriculum of transition year. Organising project work and setting goals to achieve long-term objectives may be more difficult for them than for other students.

If the transition year is well planned, it can be of enormous benefit to students. The worry that study skills may be affected because of the lack of a defined programme is offset by the development of skills in handing flexible project-related goals. This adaptability and flexibility needed for such work are skills essential for today's job market and for life.

SIZE OF SCHOOL

Large schools (schools of over 500 pupils) can provide a wider range of subjects. With more choice students may find subjects in which they can do well. Smaller schools will have less subject choice, which can be a disadvantage. On the other hand the smaller school provides an environment where each student is known by all the staff. This can have a beneficial effect on self-esteem and strengthen a feeling of being part of the school community. There may also be smaller classes. There may be less streaming.

CLASS SIZE

It is very much to the student's advantage if class sizes are small. In a small class the teacher has more time to pay individual attention to students. Maximum class size guidelines at second-level are thirty students in academic classes such as English or Maths and twenty-four for practical classes such as Science and Home Economics. In state-funded schools classes tend to be close to these numbers. Some schools try to arrange that the numbers of students in the weakest classes are smaller than in the rest of the classes of the year group. This has been helped in recent years by the allocation of resource teaching hours for special needs pupils. The number of students in classes in private schools can be lower as the private schools have additional funds to employ extra teachers.

SCHOOL ATTITUDE TO LEARNING DIFFICULTIES

Some schools can be very supportive of the needs of students with diverse learning difficulties including dyslexia and have structures in place to assist them. In meeting with the principal of a school for the first time to discuss the needs of the student, it will become apparent whether the school has a supportive attitude or not. This is the time to raise issues such as an exemption from Irish, reasonable accommodation in state exams and support services inside the school. Even if the school principal does not accede to requests, the fact that he/she is willing to discuss such issues, will indicate something about the school attitude.

The Education Act and the EPSEN Act have huge implications for access to and participation of students with disabilities in schools. Many parents speak about schools who are unwilling to take students with learning difficulties or schools that do not provide adequate support services. These two Acts have made schools more accountable and provide parents with increased rights.

One very immediate way to improve teacher awareness about dyslexia and other learning difficulties is to provide in-service training for existing teachers. Schools are allowed one day for in-service training for the whole staff during the academic year. Parents could, either themselves or through the Parents' Association, request that the school consider holding an in-service day on dyslexia or the wider topic of special educational needs. It is particularly relevant now that the legislation has stressed the role of the school in providing appropriate education for students with special needs. The Special Education Support Service (www.sess.ie) was set up in 2003 and part of its activities is the provision of such training.

ADDITIONAL TEACHING SUPPORT

The student, on entrance to second-level, may still need additional help. Such help can be provided by a learning support teacher or a resource teacher. Are such facilities available? Will the student qualify under the criteria set out in the Department of Education and Science Circulars for access to such help? Further information is included in Chapter 3.

LEVELS OF PAPERS IN STATE EXAMINATIONS

At Junior Certificate level, the subjects of Irish, English and Maths may be taken at three levels: higher, ordinary and foundation. Roughly about 40% of the students take the higher paper, 50% take the ordinary and 10% take the foundation. Students, who take the foundation or ordinary level in a subject, normally would not go on to sit the Leaving Certificate in that subject at higher level. Foundation Maths at Junior Certificate is likely to lead on to foundation level Maths at Leaving Certificate. *Foundation level Maths and Irish are not acceptable for entry to many courses and careers.* The vast majority of courses in the Institutes of Technology specify the student must have passed ordinary level Maths as well as ordinary level English or Irish at Leaving Certificate. The decision that a student drop to foundation level Maths may be taken as early as second year at second-level and can have serious career implications later on. There is no foundation paper in English at Leaving Certificate so there can be a big jump for a student to go from foundation level at Junior Certificate to Ordinary level English at Leaving Certificate level.

In all other subjects other than English, Irish and Maths in the Junior Certificate there are two levels, higher and ordinary. It is intended that the majority of students would take the higher level paper. The ordinary level paper in these subjects is more the equivalent of the foundation level in Irish, English and Maths. A student who wants to do higher level at Leaving Certificate in a particular subject should be taking a higher level paper for the Junior Certificate.

Does the school teach all levels for the Junior Certificate? If ordinary level or foundation level would be more suitable for a particular child, will there be a class at this level? Will the student be in a mixed class with two or all three levels being taught in the same classroom? This is a more difficult situation for the teacher.

Types of State examinations

In recent developments of the state examination system, there are now three distinct Leaving Certificates; the established Leaving Certificate, the Leaving Certificate Applied (LCA) and the Leaving Certificate Vocational (LCV). These will be discussed in more detail in Chapter 10.

The Junior Certificate School Programme was introduced in forty-five schools in 1996 for students whose particular needs were not adequately addressed in the broadly based Junior Certificate. This programme is intended to reach out to young people who leave school early without obtaining any qualifications. The programme involves greater student activity and specific goals are set for literacy and numeracy. It is based on the concept that all young people are capable of achieving real success in school and that they can have a positive experience of education, if the conditions are favourable. It is a way of working within the Junior Certificate which is specially designed to help young people who have had a difficult experience of school. Instead of examination grades, a student profiling system is used to measure achievement.

If parents consider that a particular type of state examination programme would suit their child, they should enquire if such a programme is being provided by the school. If the parents are interested in the student attending school which does not offer the LCA, they may consider the option of the student changing school after the Junior Certificate or transition year.

Friends

In some cases the student with learning difficulties may have difficulty making new friends easily. This may be the result of past bullying or low self-esteem. Such students might have a small number of friends. It will help the transition to second-level if they go to the same school as their friends.

Co-ed versus single sex schools

While there has been research which suggests that girls' achievement in co-ed schools may drop, having worked in a co-ed school for many years, I see no advantage in one over the other. However in the case of students with learning difficulties, there are some schools where there is a very competitive ethos either academically or on the sporting field. If the student is not achieving academically and is not participating in the major sport of the school, self-esteem may be affected. In this case I would choose either a school where there is less emphasis on competitive success or a co-ed school where, because of the wide mix of students, there are many different types of activities offered.

EXTRACURRICULAR ACTIVITIES

I have mentioned that self-esteem may be fragile in students with learning difficulties. They have experienced difficulty and failure with the academic part of the curriculum. However they can achieve success and peer recognition in other areas such as the extra-curricular activities organised by the school. Some schools put on a wide range of activities which can include sports of every type, debating, drama, organising a school bank, camera clubs and social concerns such as Amnesty International. Parents should check and see which activities are available.

However it must be remembered that often it is the student with poor self-esteem who may be reluctant to join in group activities. Information about what is available may not reach home as students are aware that parents might encourage them to participate. Parents should become aware of what is available by contacting the school. It is much easier to get a young teenager involved in school activities in First Year than it is later on in school life.

DISTANCE FROM THE HOME TO SCHOOL

Living close to the school can facilitate student's participation in extra-curricular activities. Living at a distance from the school can mean the student misses out on social life and friendships. It is more difficult to participate in many aspects of school life if the student is tied to transport timetables or is relying on parents to provide lifts.

SUMMARY

Several different factors should be considered when choosing a school. There will be no perfect school that will meet all criteria.

Parents, in consultation with the child, need to decide on what they consider to be the most important. They should then research the schools in their locality and decide on the school which will best meet their child's needs.

Below is a checklist of the points discussed in this chapter. They are not in order of importance as such prioritising will very much depend on the student's strengths and weaknesses, self-esteem, and social skills.

♦ Class placement.

♦ Choice of subjects.

♦ Irish.

♦ Discipline.

♦ Transition year.

♦ Size of school.

♦ Size of class.

♦ School attitude to learning difficulties.

♦ Learning support/ Resource teaching.

♦ Levels of papers in the Junior Certificate.

♦ Leaving Certificate and Junior Certificate Programmes provided.

♦ Friendship.

♦ Co-ed versus single sex schools.

♦ Extra-curricular activities.

♦ Distance from home to school.

Coping with Second-Level: How Parents Can Help

6

The change to second-level is a big transition point for all students. The student is moving from having one teacher all day to having several teachers in the course of a day. There is also the introduction of new subjects. There is more emphasis on examinations, both state and school-based. The vast majority of students cope well and are very positive about the move and have settled in well by mid-term. However this transition may bring more pressures for students with dyslexia. The most obvious change is that at primary-level students have had one teacher who knew them and their difficulties well. Now students may face up to nine different teachers in a day. They need to be organised to face the different demands of these teachers. The primary school curriculum concentrates on numeracy and literacy. Now new subjects appear and must be mastered. It is expected that basic skills in numeracy and literacy are in place. There is a certain curriculum to be covered in time for the state examinations.

Parental interest is a vital component in a student's progress. However there are some extremes to be avoided. Some parents can set unrealistic goals and push the student to achieve them. Others can appear to be disinterested and avoid involvement with schoolwork, perhaps because they themselves found it difficult when they were at school. (It must be remembered that dyslexia may be inherited.) Others use the student's difficulties as a reason for not making any academic demands at all. However, consistent parental support, based on a realistic knowledge of the student's ability, is invaluable. I believe it to be the most important factor in the development of students' self-esteem and ability to cope. The parents' role is essential at the start of second-level, but as students mature, they should gradually take more responsibility for their progress and should develop the appropriate study skills themselves. It is a gradual process in which the parental input diminishes as the student achieves a growing independence and mastery of the necessary skills.

The Task Force on Dyslexia recognised that the involvement of parents is central to meeting the needs of children with learning difficulties arising from dyslexia and that the parents of students with such difficulties need support and advice but that they have a major contribution to make in achieving effective outcomes.

The *Understanding Dyslexia* CD which is available in all schools contains a major section for parents and includes comprehensive advice on the following:

♦ Developing self esteem.
♦ Helping with spoken language development.
♦ Helping with reading, writing and spelling.
♦ Helping with homework.
♦ Using computers at home.
♦ Supporting the child at post-primary.
♦ Coping with challenging behaviour.

The reason why parental support is so crucial at the start of second-level is that it is important students make a successful transition from primary school. There is a major challenge in coping with all the new subjects, new teachers and the new structure of the school week. If they do not achieve some level of success, there is a risk that, as a defence mechanism, they may turn off the idea of school. As a result they may become involved in 'messing'. Parents can help them meet the challenge of second-level by using appropriate interventions from the suggestions in this chapter. Computers are not covered in this chapter as their contribution is so important that Chapter 7 is solely devoted to the topic. Certainly not all these suggestions will apply to all students. Also parents need to be consistent and keep involved throughout the school year. Trying to do everything can become very onerous and it is easy then for parental efforts to falter. It is better to do a limited amount thoroughly and maintain the effort throughout the year. Read over the suggestions and take the ideas most appropriate to your child's particular needs. In my own case I concentrated on helping with notes and structuring answers as it was the most effective use of my time and that of the twins.

HOMEWORK

Homework is very important at second-level. It consolidates learning from the classroom. When material is taught in the classroom, students hear it for the first time. It is important they understand what they are being taught at this stage. This material which is understood in class will be forgotten unless the knowledge is consolidated through homework, either written or learning. It will then be forgotten within a few weeks unless it is revised on a regular basis. A revision programme means it will stay in the mind of the student.

Homework can become a battleground, fraught with difficulties. Students with dyslexia can be quite tired at the end of a day in school more so than their peers because they must concentrate harder and simple tasks can take them longer to do. Homework may also take them a longer time to complete. If the hours needed to do homework are excessive, talk to the teacher. Long hours spent at homework will only exhaust the student further. If it is taking the student an hour to do a question that will be allocated half an hour in an exam, the teacher needs to know this.

ORGANISATION OF HOMEWORK

Homework should be done as early as possible in the evening, when students still have energy. At the weekends encourage them to do written homework on a Friday night. Some students spend a lot of time 'notting', i.e. spending time not doing the homework while at the same time feeling it hang over them like a cloud. They then feel that homework takes all night because they have been thinking about it all night.

A definite routine will help establish good work practices. Homework should be done at a desk or a table, with the books and any equipment needed near at hand. The student should not study with the television or the radio on. Mobiles should be switched off or left elsewhere. Such distractions will interfere with concentration. The student should not be interrupted for telephone calls or callers to the door. An agreement can be made that these calls can be returned when the study time is over.

Many people find it difficult to be organised and tidy but some students with dyslexia find disorganisation seriously affects their work. A work area with plenty of shelving space; a desk organiser that has a place for pens, staples, paperclips; a filing routine that puts notes into folders every day; the use of different colour folders for different subjects; a routine for clearing out the schoolbag daily and packing it at night for the following day; a study timetable and calendar on the wall; these are some ideas that will reduce chaos and muddle. They should use the class timetable to check their bag for the next day. With the lack of order that can characterise their work, they are likely to forget important books and completed homework for different subjects, unless they have a checking system. Is their bag neat, or do scraps of dog-eared paper lurk in its depths? These scraps of paper often turn out to be poems given for learning or vital notes which the teacher has supplied. If they get photocopied pages from teachers, it is essential to use a good filing system.

Learning work should also be done at a desk. Some students find pacing up and down helps to improve concentration but the student should never resort to lying on a bed. It is all too easy to relax and allow the mind to drift off.

Each school will have its own guidelines for homework. I recommend an hour and half to two hours a night for a first year student five nights a week. This will increase in later years. This includes time for written homework, learning homework and revision. It can be helpful if parents and students talk about the demands of homework in the August prior to entry and set out agreed timetables which specify where and when homework is to be done. This can reduce conflict later. Often the scenario is that in October or November, parents get exasperated with or worried about a student who is doing half an hour of homework and claiming there is no more to be done. If parents can refer back to the agreed programme, it will help resolve the conflict. From the students' point of view, they benefit from having clear guidelines on what they should do.

Some students find it very difficult to set goals for homework. Parents should ensure students keep a homework notebook. It can help if they list all the classes they have in a particular day and write the homework beside the name of the subject. Some teachers write homework on the blackboard, other teachers call it out. Some homework will be written, some will be oral. All should be entered into the homework notebook. The homework notebook can also be used as a diary and a reminder system for projects and other such tasks. As a student may be disorganised, it is helpful if all the deadlines, exam dates and other events in life are in one diary.

HANDWRITING AND LAYOUT

With written homework, is it the best quality students can do or is it carelessly done? If you think it can be improved, try to set higher standards for them. Ask them to proof-read their answers. Reading the work aloud will help identify omissions, grammar and spelling problems. Some students may not be able to read their own work because of their poor handwriting, so what chance does the teacher have?

If handwriting is particularly bad, the major problems can include:

- ◆ The backs of the letters are not aligned but go off in all directions.
- ◆ Letters like 'a, d, g, o, b,' are not closed.
- ◆ The letters wander above and below the line.
- ◆ Letters like m, w, u, v, n, r, are not clearly formed, so they all look the same.

It can help if the student tries to correct one of these problems at a time. Doing this can greatly improve the legibility of the handwriting. Using good quality paper for writing can help as well.

Check the layout of Maths. Are the columns of figures straight? Often in Maths and Business Studies, mistakes are made because the columns of figures are not aligned or figures are illegible.

All this checking may seem very onerous for parents. It is, in the beginning, but it is by the consistency of the checking that standards improve. Over time, a routine will become established and the student will adopt many of the practices automatically which means the parents' role will reduce.

Learning Work

Many students consider homework to be the written work given by teachers. The teachers *will* find out if the written work is not done and there may be punishment work given. However it may be possible for the student to avoid doing some of the learning work given since it can be more difficult for teachers to check that this work is done by all students.

I see learning work as the key to success at second-level. It is mainly the work learnt by students that will be tested in the house and state examinations. The first mistake many students make is to think learning work is less important than written and to avoid doing it. The next mistake is to think learning or memorising happens by 'reading over' the text several times. This is a very common error. Reading over a chapter of history twice does not mean that it is learnt and that key points will be remembered. Students need to think about what they are going to learn and set out a clearly defined goal, e.g., 'I will learn the six causes and five effects of river erosion'. They must then use notes or make notes. These notes are then memorised.

It may also help at the end of the study period if parents ask a question or two on the topics covered that night. They do not need to understand the material, just open a page and ask a question based on that page. This technique may be helpful to the students by improving the motivation and quality of study because they know their work will be checked. Also the actual verbal recitation of what they have learned can reinforce the material learnt and help with verbal expression.

Students may have a preferred style of learning based on their own strengths. The Theory of Multiple Intelligences was proposed by Dr. Howard Gardner. It recognises that each person has a different learning style and learns at a different pace. Knowing which intelligence is stronger enables people to select learning styles that work for them. For some it is relatively easy to understand how a flower grows but it is immensely difficult to understand and use a musical instrument. For others music might be easy but playing football is difficult. Gardner originally outlined seven types of intelligences:

♦ Linguistic intelligence: a sensitivity to the meaning and order of words.

♦ Logical-mathematical intelligence: ability in mathematics and other complex logical systems.

♦ Musical intelligence: the ability to understand and create music.

♦ Spatial intelligence: the ability to "think in pictures," to perceive the visual world accurately, and recreate (or alter) it in the mind or on paper.

♦ Bodily-kinesthetic intelligence: the ability to use one's body in a skilled way, for self-expression or toward a goal.

♦ Interpersonal intelligence: an ability to perceive and understand other individuals — their moods, desires, and motivations.

♦ Intrapersonal intelligence: an understanding of one's own emotions.

♦ Later Gardner identified an eighth intelligence, the naturalist intelligence.

Some people display strengths in more than one or two areas of multiple intelligences and it is sometimes difficult to determine which intelligence is a real strength. However, by using a variety of methods when learning, learning needs are more likely to be met. There are websites which have quizzes to enable students identify their own strengths. These include www.homeworktips.about.com and www.ldpride.net.

Note-taking

Discussion of learning brings up the subject of note-taking. The ability to extract key points is a critical skill at second-level. Good notes make learning the text much easier and also can help in formulating answers as students have a structure around which they can organise their thinking. Students with dyslexia can find note-taking difficult for a number of reasons: poor reading skills, the readability levels of the textbooks, the volume and size of the texts and a lack of ability to summarise.

If they are not good at making their own notes, there are books of revision notes for some subjects. These are invaluable. They provide the key points a student needs to learn. These are available in schoolbook shops, both for Leaving Certificate and Junior Certificate levels for most subjects. At Junior Certificate level, History, Geography, Business Studies, Religion, Home Economics and Science are available. It can be extremely useful to obtain these notes at the beginning of junior cycle or senior cycle. There are notes in some subjects available on the website www.skoool.ie.

When taking notes from a written text, students should first think about the purpose of the notes and what information they want to extract from the text. For any student a mass of closely written pages of notes makes revision more difficult than it should be. A mistake many students make is that their notes are far too long. They lift complete chunks of the text and include virtually everything from the main book. Notes should be short, precise, stressing the main points only. Notes should be about a third of the length of the text from which they have been taken, preferably even shorter. Layout and presentation of notes can help all students but in particular some students with dyslexia, who, on account of good visual memory skills, may be able to hold the graphic image of the notes in their mind and work to recall the content of the notes from this image. Here are some ideas to help make notes clearer:

- Leave plenty of space, particularly margins.
- Use alternative lines of the page.
- Use different colours to highlight names and points to be remembered.
- Use headings and sub-headings.
- No need for full sentences, just put down the key words.
- Numbering of relevant points can help their recall.
- Use of mind maps to show the interrelationships between facts.
- Organise notes, so there is an index at the beginning and each page is numbered.
- Mnemonics can help recall. An example of a mnemonic from my own school days is FATDAD, for the six counties of Northern Ireland, Fermanagh Antrim, Tyrone, Derry, Armagh, and Down.

The technique of mindmaps can help students make notes and see connections between topics. This can help learning. Tony Buzan has written widely on the techniques involved in mindmapping. The website www.buzanworld.com is very informative and includes examples of mindmaps.

Two other websites that may be useful are

www.skoool.ie. This site has study notes and solutions for the Leaving Certificate and Junior Certificate subjects. Some subjects are presented interactively. It also has career information.

www.homeworktips.about.com. This site is designed to help students develop a study plan.

The Dyslexia Association of Ireland runs examination preparation classes in Dublin for students taking the Leaving Certificate and Junior Certificate. These courses are very useful. The content includes study skills and English skills. There is a waiting list for places. Contact DAI for further details

TAPES AND VIDEOS

Some students will find it useful if their notes are taped, particularly if their aural memory skills are good. The student is then obtaining the information through the eye and the ear at the same time. It has been proven that when a student hears and sees what is being read, it can improve recall by up to 40% (British Dyslexia Association). It might come down to parents actually taping the notes themselves or perhaps a group of parents sharing the task of taping. It is of more benefit to tape notes rather than the full textbook as it is the key points the student needs to be able to recall.

There have been major developments in the provision of alternative formats for learning materials. In 2007 the Dyslexia Association of Ireland, AHEAD and the National Council for the Blind were involved in a pilot project on use of alternative formats for printed material. A Leaving Certificate Geography text book was put onto DAISY format and students were given the CD and CD player. They were able to use the CD on the computer where all the maps and illustrations were available while the text was read aloud. The

CD differed from the usual talking book as it corresponded exactly to the textbook and students were able to pinpoint a particular chapter, page or heading immediately. An evaluation of the project showed that the students found it useful and easy to use and would use more such books if they were available. It is hoped to persuade educational publishers to make disks available with text books, either included in the price which would be a little higher for every book or to be purchased separately with a copy of the text. Since the information is available digitally it could be also be converted to MP3 format. These formatted books will provide a powerful learning aid for students.

Tapes and videos can be useful in teaching the English curriculum. In Junior Certificate English the teacher has a wide choice of material. If the choice of novels includes those available on tape, it may be helpful to students. They can both listen and read at the same time. This will help them recognise unfamiliar words. For some students it is so laborious to decipher a page of text that the storyline is lost. Tapes help to overcome this. Ask the teacher to consider choosing texts which are available on tape. However it is important that the text and the tape mirror each other. There are abridged versions of books available on tape that would not be the same as the written version. In the Leaving Certificate English course, videos and tapes of texts are available. Such aids make the students very familiar with the text, the story and the characters but it does not replace reading the text.

Tapes of novels are a way to widen students' information and stimulate their imagination. These students often do not read for pleasure. Using tapes of novels gives them access to literature that other students of their age have read. The library service has many tapes available. Long car journeys are a perfect opportunity to use them.

Tapes and videos can also be beneficial in teaching other subjects. Students with dyslexia benefit from multi-sensory teaching. The difficulty is finding tapes and videos relevant to the curriculum of the different subjects. During term time RTE Network 2 have educational programmes on throughout the day. Topics covered include Science, Geography and History.

SPELLING

If spelling is a difficulty, students should keep a spelling notebook in which they write any new words they meet in each subject and their meaning. Students then learn these spellings by heart. It is often the new words or names that students will find difficult to recall. The revision of the vocabulary notebook just prior to an exam can aid the recall of these terms.

Some aids to spelling have been developed. Franklin Spellmasters are electronic gadgets similar to a personal organiser. The student can spell a word and it will be checked phonetically and, if spelt incorrectly, an alternative spelling is suggested. There are a variety of these aids available, some with a thesaurus and/or a dictionary. Computers have spell-check programmes and help the student reduce spelling errors.

ESSAY-WRITING

Essay writing can pose particular problems for the student with dyslexia. Frequently parents report that students may sit for half an hour and be unable to start to write an essay whereas homework in other subjects does not pose the same difficulties. Essay writing is a complex task and the student may have difficulty in some or all of the following: understanding the title, finding the ideas, organising ideas and thoughts, finding the words to express these thoughts, spelling the words and then punctuation and handwriting. Students can cope better if they take each of these in turn.

The first thing is to read the title of the essay and make sure that it is understood. Pay attention to the key words in the title. There are certain key words that occur constantly in questions and it is surprising how many students do not know their exact meaning. See Fig. 5.1 for terminology used in questions.

Fig 5.1 Terminology Used In Questions

ANALYSE	Break into its component parts, discuss and show interrelations.
ARGUE	Make a case, using appropriate evidence, either for or against the issue.

ASSESS	Consider the value or importance of something, showing positive and negative points and give your own point of view.
COMPARE	Identify features that two or more things have in common.
CONTRAST	Identify differences between two or more things.
CRITICISE	Judge the value or truth of a topic, showing your reasons.
DEFINE	Explain something in sufficient detail for it to be distinguishable from similar things.
DESCRIBE	Outline the main aspects of an idea, or show how a thing would appear to the five senses: taste, sight, touch, smell, sound. The five questions (how, why, who, where and when), will provide a mechanism to describe some events.
ENUMERATE	List or number points, possibly using a sentence to describe each.
EVALUATE	Judge the value or importance of something, showing positive and negative aspects.
EXPLAIN	Show how things work or the sequence in their development. Describing could be part of this.
IDENTIFY	Show clearly the key features of a topic.
ILLUSTRATE	Similar to explain but should be accompanied by relevant drawings, diagrams, etc.
PROVE	Show the truth of a proposition, by presenting evidence to support your argument.
SUMMARISE	Reduce the text down to main points.
TRACE	Show the sequence of events or the interrelationships between topics.

This list is a guide to the customary meaning of these words.

The next stage is to plan the essay. In a narrative type essay which may be given in Junior Cycle, the questions students should ask themselves are Who? Where? When? What? How? Why? and what was the result? This will help structure the essay in a coherent manner.

Some essays are descriptive. A device to help students include more description in what they write, is to think of the five senses and write about the effect of the particular scene on each of the senses. An essay based on a description of a stormy day at sea could use this device as follows:

- Sight: what the clouds and sea look like, size of waves, the white foam, spray.
- Hearing: howl of the wind, crash of waves, seagulls crying.
- Smell: the odours of the sea spray.
- Feel: the cold touch of the wind, wetness of the rain and spray, the feeling of being blown along.
- Taste: the salty taste in the mouth.

In essays where they have to discuss or give opinions, they should take a sheet of paper and brainstorm the topic by writing down all the points that come into their head in any order. Then they should group linked ideas. This will help them develop the main outline of the essay, showing ideas they want to include. It will also help to organise the format of the essay. Once this is done, it is easier to see the structure of the essay and the sequence of ideas. Parents may be able to help here by checking to see that the essay is in logical order and is related to the title of the essay. This will help with paragraphing. Each paragraph should deal with a separate point. The plan should have a clear introduction, development of the topic and a conclusion.

Having the master plan ready reduces the number of tasks students now face. The thinking and structuring has been done, they must find the words to express their ideas. Thinking about what they want to say and expressing themselves aloud may help them find the English they need. A thesaurus is invaluable in finding the exact word.

Spelling is the next hurdle. It is difficult to suggest a way of handling this. Should students look up spellings of which they are unsure and interrupt the flow of writing or should spelling be checked at the end and then be corrected? The answer to this depends on what works best for each student. Many students feel that if they stop to think about a spelling it can halt the creative flow. It is important to continue to write and get the ideas down. Mistakes in punctuation and spelling can be picked up if the essay is read out aloud on completion.

It is important that handwriting is legible, particularly if the student has to write in examinations and does not have access to computers. If the writing cannot be read, marks will be lost. Perhaps rewriting an essay after the thinking, spelling and punctuation have been completed will produce a more legible end-product. It is, however, very time-consuming and frustrating. Of course, use of a word processor helps with spelling, grammar, presentation and editing.

WRITTEN EXPRESSION

The ability to express points is a key skill not only in English but also in other subjects. The Junior Certificate examination format suits students with dyslexia because in many of the subjects there are a series of brief questions in which they are asked to write short answers to demonstrate they know the facts. Handwriting, spelling and composition are less important in this type of answering. There is an enormous jump in the standard of answers needed at Leaving Certificate level. In many subjects at this level students must be able to construct a longer essay-type answer and show what they know. This can pose a challenge to the student who may find longer written answers involving organisation of information difficult.

The work of students with dyslexia when answering such essay type questions is often criticised for being too short. Use of guidelines or a prepared structure can help the student write more. Here are some examples.

- ♦ Frequently in English students may be asked to discuss the traits of a character in a play such as Romeo in the play Romeo and Juliet. A student may write an answer such as 'He is romantic, brave, impatient and a good friend'. The student may believe the question is answered, but in reality, instead of one line of an answer, the teacher expects a page at least and so marks are lost. However, if the student knows he/she must think up four different characteristics of Romeo and for each one, to describe two incidences in the play where Romeo showed this trait, the answer will be much longer and more comprehensive. By the time he/she has included an introduction and conclusion, the answer is much closer to the teacher's expectation.

♦ Another example is from History. Students may be asked to write about the life of a person in an ancient civilisation or a monk in medieval times. A list of items, which might apply to such a question, will prompt them to write more. Such a list could include: daily routine, transport, food, clothes, housing, power, crafts, burial, education and religion.

♦ In writing an English essay or in answering questions that require a personal response, the stumbling block for some students is that they feel they must give their own experience or opinion. If they are writing an English essay, they are free to use their imagination and not be limited by their own experience or a real event. If they find it difficult to formulate a personal response to a poetry question, it can be helpful to realise that so long as their answer is relevant to the question that it does not necessarily have to be their opinion.

READING

Reading is a key skill at second-level. Most students with dyslexia have some reading skills but they need to pick up on speed and stamina. Such skills help them to access the information in textbooks across the curriculum. They often do not like reading. It can be so laborious that the story can get lost when trying to decipher the text. Yet if their reading is to develop, they must practise. It can be difficult to get books to suit the student. Books with a suitable reading level may have a very babyish content. Again the library service has books that may help. Some libraries have adult literacy schemes and have books with adult content, which have been abridged and the vocabulary simplified. These books can be graded for various reading levels. Penguin Books have an excellent range of such books and many are based on topics that will interest reluctant readers such as footballers or the story of films they may have seen. A routine of doing twenty minutes reading daily even throughout the summer can help develop and maintain reading skills.

When reading texts or suggested background reading, students should read actively. This means they begin by being clear about the purpose of the reading. What exactly do they want to find out? They should read with a pen in their hand, so they can take note of major points. Making notes will also help with concentration. The student should check new words in a dictionary or thesaurus.

REVISION

Revision is an important element of work done at home. Written homework, learning homework and revision are the three ways which will help students achieve their potential. All are necessary. Written and learning homework will be given by the teacher. Both written work and learning by heart will ensure work done in class is understood and consolidate the material covered. However if students do not revise, they will forget the content relatively quickly. Regular revision ensures that it is remembered. Part of the student's study timetable should include revision plans. A plan should be made out showing the subjects to be revised after homework each night. An example is given below for a Junior Certificate student.

MONDAY	TUESDAY	WEDNESDAY	THURSDAY	FRIDAY
History	Science	Maths	History	Business Studies
English	Irish	French	Science	Geography
Geography	Maths	Business Studies	English	Irish & French

The student in first year should plan to do two hours work a night. If homework takes an hour the rest of the time would be divided between the subjects for revision. If the student has a lot of homework one night, then the revision could be included in another night's work or the weekend. Adapt it to the student's personal schedule. If there is a scouts' meeting or a sports session one night, leave that night free of revision.

Setting goals is important in revision too. The student should make out a clear target to be learnt in the revision. The important aspect of revision is not the amount of time but the goals that have been met. A student may waste two hours sitting looking over books and know very little at the end of the session. An example of such targeted revision could read as follows:

♦ In Maths, revision of three theorems and do ten examples from the textbook based on them.

♦ In Geography, revision of rock types, how to recognise them, where they occur, and what are their uses.

♦ In History, revision of how the monks lived in a medieval monastery, under the headings of work, food, manuscripts and clothes.

Coming closer to exams, revision becomes even more important. About six weeks before the exam, check that students have the list of topics on which the examination will be based. This could be done on a single sheet of paper with a column for each subject. They may need help from teachers to do this as the student with dyslexia can have difficulty in quantifying and organising the work to be done. They then plan to cover a sixth of each subject list per week until the exams start. As they revise a topic they mark it off the list, so that they can see their progress on the chart.

This can also help reduce the anxiety before an exam. The students will feel they are in control and they will have completely covered the course before the exam. This feeling of control helps minimise stress and anxiety. Stress is unfortunately part of the educational system. However, for students with dyslexia, stress and time pressures can make their particular problems worse and their thoughts can jump about and lack order. A clear revision plan, with clear goals, helps in keeping stress levels under control. Other well-known stress management techniques such as healthy eating and regular exercise also help.

PROJECT WORK

Projects can cause problems for students with dyslexia. These can include: difficulty in sourcing materials, in reading widely to pick out relevant points, in organising the structure of the project and in its presentation. Parents can provide vital assistance in all these tasks. It can give students a sense of achievement to undertake a project and bring it to completion. When they are given the project outline, help them work out a time frame for the various parts of it and set a completion date. They are learning valuable skills in organising projects and work as they come to terms with their time goals. Selecting and narrowing the reading they have to do can help them as well. Computer skills are very valuable in project work as it helps in the organisation, presentation, layout and spelling of the final result. It means that these students can produce a project that looks professional.

CONTACT WITH THE SCHOOL

Parents should ensure the school has a full profile of the student by sending in copies of psycho-educational assessments. It is helpful if they make suggestions based on their experience on what might work best with the student and that these are as specific as possible. Examples of such recommendations could be that notes be photocopied, that the student use revision handbooks or that the student be allowed to produce homework done on a computer. It can strengthen the parents' requests if suggestions such as these are backed by recommendations in the assessment.

However even if parents have given a copy of the psycho-educational assessment to the school principal, they should not assume that all teachers will be informed of its contents. Schools are large complex organisations and all relevant members of staff may not be informed. The student will have up to ten teachers each year. I suggest making out a sheet explaining the difficulties of the student and any recommendations on which teaching methods might work best for the student. Parents could arrange to see the teachers individually and give them this sheet. Parents could also send it to the substitute teacher if a teacher is going to be absent for a period of time. If reading aloud in class is a major difficulty for a student, teachers need to know this on the first day the student is in the class so that they will delay asking him/her to read aloud. On that first day, the students coming from many different feeder schools are judging each other. If the student cannot read aloud, it will be part of this evaluation. However after a few weeks, when the student has found his/her place in the class, the fact that he/she cannot read with ease, will not have the same impact with peers.

Parents should check if the student would benefit from an exemption from Irish and ask the school if the student qualifies under the regulations set out by the Department of Education and Science. They should contact the school to discuss whether to apply for reasonable accommodation in the state examinations for their child. If the application for reasonable arrangements is turned down, there is an appeals procedure. If reasonable accommodations are appropriate for the state examinations, will they be provided in house examinations?

OTHER ACTIVITIES

I have mentioned in the first chapter that self-esteem may be low in students with dyslexia. At second-level they may find subjects that they have an aptitude for and will enjoy. However many subjects still have a high verbal content and the student may be struggling and still experiencing a sense of failure. Self-esteem gives students the confidence to try out new experiences and to feel they can manage life. A belief in one's self is the key to the transition to an independent adult life. It can be fostered by the student being involved in extra-curricular activities and becoming competent in them. Involvement in sport, obtaining awards such as scouting badges, involvement in community activity such as visiting old people; developing skills such as photography or life-saving; being competent on a musical instrument; getting work experience; these are all activities which can foster self-confidence. Parents can play a role in getting students involved, particularly at an early age. As the student goes through the teenage years, the influence of parents diminishes. It should be remembered that all of these activities contribute to a Curriculum Vitae.

KEEPING GOING

Throughout this chapter I have mentioned ways parents can help the student. These all take time and effort over a long period of time. It can be very fatiguing. It is easy to start the year with good resolutions but to keep going consistently through the long months can be tough. It must be remembered that these students have to work so hard in comparison to their peers simply to keep up with the class. They often have extra classes. A piece of learning might take them twice as long to do as other students. Writing an essay can be a strenuous exercise for them, whereas for another student it can be a pleasure. They can be tired and frustrated at times. And for all their hard work, they might not get the satisfaction of good grades. Parents also can feel the strain of providing consistent support. Sometimes, as a result, homework can become a flashpoint for irritation. This should be avoided. Such confrontations can undo a lot of good work done on self-esteem.

Parents must realise that they can make a contribution to the student's learning and progress that is irreplaceable. No one else can be there everyday on a one-to-one basis. However it is important for parents to realise they are only human and can only do so much. They should pick out the key three or four ways to help that they think most relevant and concentrate on those. I had to learn to do this over the years. My key points were note-taking and goal-setting. There are other suggestions in this chapter which would have benefited the boys but neither they nor I had the energy to pursue them.

The most important contribution parents can make is the development of a loving, secure relationship where the students are prized for themselves and not their results and are given a feeling of support and parental backing.

Giving parental support is not a static process. At the beginning parents may be very involved in goal setting, checking homework, setting out revision plans, helping with projects but the intention should be that students would develop these skills and would learn to apply these skills independently. How quickly this happens depends on many variables, such as the student's own abilities, maturity and relationship with parents. It is a process that develops over a number of years. It is important to see the parents' help as a part of this process which will end up with the students taking responsibility and developing their own skills. If such gradual hand-over from parent to student does not take place, the help is a crutch and the student will become dependent on it.

Computers and Information Technology

7

Computers and information technology are of enormous help for all students but, in particular, provide essential and significant help to students with dyslexia. Such help is invaluable and this generation of students is very fortunate in having information and communications technology available.

How Computers Can Help Students With Dyslexia

Computers can provide assistance in the following ways:

- ◆ Increased motivation as computers may be fun to use.

- ◆ Programmes that adapt to proceed at the student's own pace so boredom and frustration do not set in. There can also be immediate feedback rather than the student having to wait for the teacher's corrections.

- ◆ Assistive technologies where the computer may help students carry out tasks that they find difficult such as spelling, reading or writing.

- ◆ Programmes which help diagnose dyslexic characteristics.

- ◆ Word processors allow students to present work clearly and legibly. This can help achievement and self-esteem. It also helps students in completing work faster and allows for editing. Spelling and grammar checks are available.

- ◆ Programmes to help the student gain literacy and numeracy skills. Students with dyslexia benefit from multi-sensory teaching and repetition, both of which computers provide.

- ◆ Programmes which read any text on the screen aloud including the internet.

◆ Programmes which help develop study skills or organisation skills.

◆ Speech recognition software so the student can dictate to the computer and obtain a typed copy.

◆ Access to websites on the topic of study skills or which provide study notes for subjects in the Leaving or Junior Certificate. These study notes can now be read aloud, so the student is seeing and hearing the information.

With so many programmes and products available, it is easy to become confused with the choice. Computer software is often expensive and comes packaged, so it is difficult to find out prior to purchase if a product is suitable. Ways of obtaining practical experience of the software include advice from teachers, demonstrations of software at conferences/exhibitions or demonstration disks from suppliers or downloads from the Internet. Students may use a particular software package in school or in a Dyslexia Association of Ireland workshop and find it of benefit. The web sites listed at the end of this chapter also provide a means of obtaining current information.

VAT can be claimed back on the purchase of computers/assistive technology for home/personal use, via Form VAT 61A

KEYBOARDING SKILLS

At the present time, the main method of inputting information into the computer is keyboarding. To be able to use a word processor effectively, touch-typing skills or at least keyboard familiarity using eight fingers are needed. It takes the investment of time and effort to persevere to learn to touch-type and it is well worth the effort particularly for the student with dyslexia who is likely to benefit so much from using word processors. It is very difficult for a person who uses the two-finger approach and looks at the keys to change over to touch-typing so developing these skills as early as possible is recommended. Some students are well motivated and can learn by themselves. Others may need the discipline that comes from a course of structured learning with a teacher. Like all skills, keyboarding needs to be practised regularly if it is to develop and be maintained.

The reasonable accommodations allowed in state examinations include the use of a word processor for a small number of students. If the school is to assess whether a student would benefit from using a word processor in examinations, the student needs to be proficient in its use. This means, in the case of a Junior Certificate student, good keyboarding skills should be in place by the end of second year.

If the use of a word processor helps students to achieve, they should be allowed to produce homework, projects and house exams in this way.

The British Dyslexia Association's website has an information sheet on keyboard skills and touch-typing. It includes the criteria for choosing a touch-typing package for students with dyslexia and the names of recommended packages. One of the key recommendations is that the package should not use any 'near-words' e.g. 'hed', 'kik', as these could confuse the student with dyslexia who is trying to learn to spell correctly.

SCREENING PROGRAMMES

In 1996 the Computer Resource Centre at the University of Hull developed a diagnostic screening system called Cognitive Profiling System (CoPS) to be used in the four to six age group. It measured a child's reaction to various challenges on the computer screen. This has been developed into four programmes for different ages.

- ♦ CoPS baseline for children between four years and five years and six months.
- ♦ Lucid CoPS for children between four and eight.
- ♦ LASS Junior for individuals between eight and eleven.
- ♦ LASS Secondary for individuals between eleven and fifteen.

All four use standardised norms researched in the UK.

ASSISTIVE TECHNOLOGY

Assistive technology provides the student with help in doing tasks they find difficult. In the case of dyslexia, computer technology provides very real help for the student.

The main forms of assistive technology are:

- ♦ Word processors with spelling and grammar checks. These

enable the student to provide written material of good quality. This is particularly useful if handwriting is poor and takes a lot of effort. It can be faster and easier than writing by hand provided the student has good keyboarding skills. It is also good for self-esteem to see one's work look well. Editing and rearranging text is easy, so students do not have to rewrite laboriously to produce a final copy. This facility also helps students who have sequencing difficulties as it is easy to edit the text so as to rearrange the sequence of points. Mistakes are easy to correct as spelling and grammar checks are provided. Because the word processor minimises spelling and handwriting difficulties, students are free to concentrate on ideas and the way they want to express them. It encourages them to be more adventurous and creative. It helps the student organise work as it can be saved and filed on the computer. *Alphasmart* is a machine that does word processing only. It can hold 64 pages of material in eight separate files in its memory that can be downloaded to a printer or to a computer for filing. It has a small screen displaying four lines at a time. It is robust and relatively inexpensive.

♦ Speech recognition software. This allows the student dictate to the computer which produces a typed copy on the screen. More and more of these systems are coming on the market. The programmes need to learn the voice of the user so it takes time to train a system to an individual's voice. The user also needs training in being consistent in giving commands and punctuation instructions. Developing dictation accuracy is important for students with dyslexia, as they may have more difficulty identifying mistakes made on the screen and correcting them. A good sound card and microphone is necessary. *Dragon Naturally Speaking* is one such programme. Information sheets on speech recognition systems are available from BDA and IANSYST websites which are listed at the end of the chapter

♦ *Magnetictime* allows people to list to emails and word documents on an iPod, PDA (personal digital assistant), mobile phone or MP3 player. It stores the emails and documents similarly to how it stores music and it has a large storage capacity. It allows for the documents to played, paused, stopped, skipped back or forward and filed in playlists. It is relatively inexpensive. Its name changed in 2007 to *iAudioize*. There is another programme called *iNewscaster* which collects news, websites, podcasts and delivers them to the desktop, from where they can be transferred to iPods, MP3 players, PDAs or mobile phones. Full information on www.magnetictime.com.

♦ The programme *Kurzweil* scans written material, displays it on-screen and reads it aloud. It can be used on texts suitable for young children all the way to college students. It is easy to see how such a system can benefit the student who is learning to read, but it is also of huge benefit to second and third-level students who may have to read complicated text a number of times to extract the main points. By hearing as well as reading the text, this task can become much easier. The programme also displays and reads aloud internet documents. It is possible to scan coloured documents although there is a cheaper version of *Kurzweil* that only uses black and white. Text sections can be highlighted in different colours and users can note or extract text to produce a study outline. Users are able to read along, take notes and highlight relevant text on-screen. Language tools such as a dictionary, thesaurus and phonetic spelling capability provide additional support. The student can add notes to the text, either written or by voice. Reading speed can be adjusted to suit the student. A similar programme is *ClaroRead*.

♦ *Teasease*, *Co-Writer* and *Penfriend* support writing with features such as talking spell checkers, and word prediction which increase the speed of writing. *Clicker* is a programme which uses whole words and pictures.

♦ *Read and Write Gold* which allows text to be read back and spoken as it is typed. Words can be highlighted as they are typed. There is a phonic spell-checker which can speak the words aloud. There is a context-based word prediction facility. As the user types the first letter of a word, suggestions are made in the word prediction list. This reduces the number of keystrokes used helping with speed and sentence construction. The programme also has voice recognition software and will also read text on the screen. There is a mapping element which allows information to be sorted and stored in a graphic way.

♦ *Browsealoud* is a software solution which enables website content be spoken without the need for any software to be installed on a webserver. The solution is designed to make the website work harder by opening its content to those with literacy difficulties, an aging population and those whose first language is not English. Increasing numbers of websites have provided this facility. Further information on the website: www.browsealoud.com.

♦ *Quickionary* Reading Pen. This hand-held reading pen can scan a word or line from any printed text, display the words in large letters, read the word(s) aloud, and define the word. It is possible to use a headset for private listening.

♦ *QuickLink* Pen is a 'Digital highlighter' for scanning information when away from the computer. It scans and stores the information and then downloads it to the PC. It is very useful for taking notes and quotes.

♦ *Electronic personal organisers* which can include a diary, spreadsheet, database, word processing facility, calculator, alarm and e-mail facility. Some students with dyslexia can tend to be disorganised. Structuring their life with the use of such an organiser helps in recall of important facts and deadlines.

♦ *Franklin electronic dictionaries*: If students want to know how a word is spelt and they are not working at a computer, they just key in the word that they are looking for. Franklins will work from even quite strange spelling and offer the correct spelling. Many also have dictionaries and thesauruses to help make sure that the students are using the right word. Some of the more expensive dictionaries even read words and definitions out loud.

♦ *E-Books*: the student gets the text in electronic form and can control the typeface (font), foreground and background colour and type size. It is possible to read E-Books on computer or PDAs.

♦ *Alternative Format learning materials.* When students with dyslexia can access learning materials in alternative formats, they are given tools to help them learn. Students can gain access through books on DAISY format on CD or MP3. These are formatted in the same page sequence as the book, so if the teacher calls a page number, the student enters the number and immediately accesses the page. The student can hear and see the text at the same time. A pilot project based on a Leaving Certificate Geography text was carried out in Ireland in 2007.

PROGRAMMES WHICH SUPPORT LEARNING

Examples of some of the software available are detailed below. Again the websites (in particular the British Dyslexia Association) listed at the end of this chapter have comprehensive information on programmes.

♦ *Wordshark* combines the excitement of computer games with learning to spell and read. It offers twenty six different games that use sound, graphics and text to teach and reinforce word recognition and spelling.

♦ *Starspell* helps develop spelling skills from the young child to teenagers. It uses the Look-Cover-Write-Check strategy. Every word is spoken and many have pictures. It is possible to create personal lists of words.

♦ *Numbershark* is a programme to help anyone improve basic numeracy. It uses a wide range of computer games to develop number skills. It offers thirty different games covering addition, subtraction, multiplication and division in ways which add meaning and understanding to these operations. It is suitable for ages six to adult.

♦ *Inspiration* is a programme to help students in structuring written work. People with dyslexia often prefer to think in pictures rather than in words. They like to use idea mapping – to build a visual map of ideas using pictures, colours, shapes and relationships. They use the technique for note-taking, remembering information and organising ideas for written work. Inspiration allows the student build pictures on screen and then convert the image to a linear outline. The outline can be copied into the word processor and used as a basis for writing.

♦ *Wordswork* is a multi-sensory programme on study skills. It was designed primarily for undergraduates with dyslexia but is very relevant for students at second-level and for adults who want to improve their skills before going back to formal education. It uses graphics, voice-overs, colour and humour to develop a variety of language skills which students with dyslexia (and others) need to address. Topics covered include essay writing, exam revision and time management.

The benefits which computers offer are clearly illustrated by a student with dyslexia who did a BA in Social Care in DIT. She described her experience of going to college in the following terms.

'Since I started college I have never been happier. I've gone from total frustration and upset to loving my life. I do find the workload difficult and still have a problem keeping up with notes during lectures, as I get stuck on a spelling. When trying to spell a word I often lose a full paragraph of notes, as the lecturer cannot wait for me. This is frustrating especially since lecturers don't give out notes. Life has become so much easier due to the support as well as the fact that I received, as assistive technology, the Kurzweil 3000 and Dragon Naturally Speaking. The Kurzweil 3000 reads the material I need aloud to me. This gives me independence as I don't have to rely on Mam and it saves me a lot of time. Reading a chapter for college used to take me a lot of time, as I needed to read through it for difficult words, then had to look up these words, write in their meanings and read it through again to get an idea of the text. Finally I had to read it to pick up the relevant information and take notes. Now instead of three to four hours, it takes me forty-five minutes to an hour as I can speedread with the Kurzweil, highlight the relevant parts, look up as many words as I need to, cut and edit to make out revision notes, all at the same time. The Dragon Naturally Speaking also saves me time as usually I spend so much time concentrating on my spelling that I lose my train of thought and cannot focus on the correct way to phrase my words. Now I dictate what I need to write, without worrying about spelling. The words appear on the screen, and after a few adjustments, it is ready to be printed. All this has helped me so much that for the first time in my life, I passed my exams for the last two years with all honours.'

SOURCES OF INFORMATION

British Dyslexia Association (BDA) Website:
www.bdadyslexia.org.uk

- ◆ Information sheets on
- ◆ Keyboard skills and touch-typing
- ◆ Supporting literacy with ICT
- ◆ Supporting writing with ICT
- ◆ Study Skills
- ◆ Speech recognition Devices
- ◆ Small and portable devices
- ◆ Help with the workplace
- ◆ Help finding a job.

IANSYST Ltd.
The White House, Fen House, Fen Road Cambridge, CB4 1UN, UK.
Website: www.dyslexic.com

National Centre for Technology in Education
Dublin City University, Dublin 9. Web: www.ncte.ie

IRISH SUPPLIERS OF ICT

Andrews Award Systems, 38 Pine Valley Park, Dublin 16.
Phone: 01 4930011 Web: www.awardsys.net

Ash Technologies, Naas, Co. Kildare.
Phone: 045 882212 Web: www.ashtech.ie

Carroll Educational Supplies
34A Lavery Avenue Park, West Dublin 12
Phone: 01 6120860 Web: www.carrollheinemann.ie

Computerspeak
Guinness Enterprise Centre, Taylor's Lane, Dublin 8
Phone: 01 4401940 Web: www.computerspeak.ie

Diskovery Educational Software
Unit 2, Waveney, Howth Harbour, Co. Dublin.
Phone: 01 8063910 Web: www.diskovery.ie

Edtech Software Ltd.
Murrisk, Westport, Co. Mayo
Phone/Fax 1850 923459 Web: www.edtech.ie

Jackson Technology
24 Kiltipper Ave, Aylesbury, Dublin 24
Phone 01 4518508/01 Web: www.jacksontechnology.com

TextHelp Systems Ltd.,
Enkalon Business Centre, 25 Randalstown Road, Antrim, B41 4LJ N.
Ireland.
Tel: 048 84942810 Website: www.texthelp.com

Support Services at Second Level

8

I have worked as a second-level teacher since 1982 and from my experience I believe that, at this level, there is a lack of knowledge about dyslexia, a lack of support structures and a lack of information on effective teaching strategies for students affected by dyslexia as well as other learning difficulties. Much more progress has been made at primary and third-level. As part of the training on the new curriculum at primary level, all teachers have received in-service on the topics of special education. The improvement in services for students with dyslexia and other difficulties at third level has been the result of the work of AHEAD and the development of the Disability Support Service in the colleges.

However, at second level, the vast majority of serving teachers have received little or no in-service or pre-service training on the topic of dyslexia or special needs. Such lack of training has resulted in underdeveloped services and a lack of knowledge about teaching strategies in this sector of education. Hopefully, now that the Special Education Support Service now is offering courses to schools, this will change. There have also been a number of significant documents which point the way for schools in developing school policies and support structures. The challenge now is to move from documents to implementation in schools.

The comments above do not refer to learning support teachers and resource teachers who have had specialised training and in-service courses on the topic of dyslexia and other learning difficulties. Such teachers have extensive knowledge of how to teach literacy and numeracy skills to students including those affected by dyslexia. Many students with dyslexia have benefited enormously from the invaluable contribution made to their progress by such teaching.

However one or two teachers in a school with such expertise do not change the ethos within a school. This takes whole-school planning and leadership from school management.

INCLUSIVE WHOLE-SCHOOL POLICIES AND PROCEDURES

The goal of inclusion is to create a framework where differences between individuals are accommodated. Inclusion is broader than integration. Integration means the burden of adaptation is often placed on the student who learns differently. Inclusion, on the other hand, implies the diverse needs and learning differences of all students are accommodated and appropriate structures and arrangements are adopted to enable each student to achieve maximum benefit.

The Post-primary Guidelines on Inclusion of Students with Special Educational Needs sets out the process of planning for inclusion at a whole-school level in detail. The school's mission statement and the policies and procedures set out in the school plan are pivotal in establishing a positive agenda for inclusion. Schools are advised to examine and, if appropriate, revise their culture or ethos, values, mission statement, policies, procedures, management style, organisational arrangements, curriculum content and approaches to learning and teaching with a view to establishing a school climate and curriculum that are fully inclusive. The guidelines acknowledge the significant challenge this presents for post-primary schools. Certain factors such as the nature of the syllabus, state examinations, the organisation of classes, timetabling and conflicting priorities can act as constraints.

Significant issues also arise for individual teachers in providing appropriate education for students in their classrooms. These issues include the management of time, preparation of teaching, the learning and application of new teaching techniques for differentiation and individualised learning, the maintenance of adequate pace in order to cover long syllabi and the pressures and expectations that arise in the preparation of students for state examinations. All teachers require the support of school management to enable them to access the in-career development opportunities that are available.

The whole-school policies and procedures that such planning should cover include:

♦ School enrolment policy.

♦ School attendance policy and procedures for encouraging attendance from students with poor attendance.

♦ Promotion of a school ethos including the acceptance of diversity.

♦ Procedures for the transfer of students from the primary sector.

♦ Arrangements to facilitate the transfer of students to post-school settings.

♦ Procedures for a staged approach in identifying and responding to students with low achievement or special educational needs.

♦ Parental involvement.

♦ Individual Education Plans.

♦ Models of organisation for interventions such as additional teaching support.

♦ Procedures to allow students select appropriate programmes and suitable subject choices.

EXEMPTION FROM IRISH

Irish is a compulsory subject and all students in Ireland have to study it as far as Leaving Certificate. Rule 46 of the Rules and Programme for Secondary Schools allows some students an exemption from Irish. One of the grounds for such an exemption is that it is given to students who function intellectually at average or above-average level but have a specific learning difficulty of such a degree of severity that they fail to achieve expected levels of attainment in basic language skills in the mother tongue. The guideline is that the student is in the lowest ten per cent of achievement in their mother tongue on a standardised test.

In most schools an alternative subject to Irish is rarely provided. This means the student has one less subject in state examinations and also has extra free time. Many students with an exemption end up at the back of the Irish classroom doing homework. If the school could provide something constructive to do in this time such as giving the student English reading, extra tuition or extra computer time, it would be a positive use of this free time.

PROVISION OF ADDITIONAL TEACHING SUPPORT

Additional teaching support for students comes either as learning support or resource teaching hours.

Learning support provision

In the *Learning Support Guidelines*, published by the Department of Education and Science in 2000, the criteria for the provision of such support at primary level were clarified. The Guidelines set out that supplementary teaching be provided to students who have not yet achieved basic competence in English and Mathematics i.e. those performing below the 10th percentile on nationally standardised tests of literacy and numeracy. At second-level while there are no such published guidelines, most of the learning support would be directed at students with similar numeracy and literacy levels. This means that students with dyslexia, whose scores are higher than this, may not benefit from learning support.

Resource teaching

Resource teaching hours are allocated to post-primary schools for the support of individual students who have been assessed as having special education needs.

In 2005 the National Council for Special Education took on the responsibility for processing applications for additional teaching support, special needs assistants support, assistive technology and school transport for these students. The National Council for Special Education circular NCSE 02/05 and the Department of Education circular 01/05 set our the position regarding submitting applications for any of the above

The disabilities listed in the circular include:

♦ Physical disability.

♦ Hearing or visual impairment.

♦ Emotional disturbance.

♦ Severe emotional disturbance.

- Borderline/mild general learning difficulty.
- Mild general learning difficulty.
- Moderate general learning difficulty.
- Severe/profound general learning difficulty.
- Autism/autistic spectrum disorders.
- **Specific learning disability.**
- Assessed syndrome.
- Specific speech and language disorder.
- Multiple disabilities.

To qualify under the heading Specific Learning Difficulty, students must have been assessed by a psychologist as follows:

- Being of average intelligence or higher.
- Having a degree of learning disability specific to the basic skills in reading, writing or mathematics which places them at or below the 2nd percentile on suitable standardised norm-referenced tests.

The application for resource teaching hours by the schools is made in February/March. The school should therefore inform parents of incoming students that psycho-educational assessment reports should be sent into the school by the January prior to entry. This means that in the case of students for whom resource teaching is appropriate, the school can apply in time and have the additional resources in place by September of entry. The NCSE target is that schools will be informed of the decision re applications by the end of April.

Applications are made by the principal of the school and must include details of the pupil(s), details of disabilities, an assessment by the principal of the quantity and type of additional resources required and copies of assessment reports. Parental consent is needed and the PPS number of the student must be supplied. In the case of students with specific learning difficulty, the assessment must be less than four years old. Additional testing is required if it is older than this.

Use of additional teaching support

The Post-primary Guidelines for the Inclusion of Students with Special Educational Needs state that it is critical that a school's allocation of resource-teacher hours for special educational needs is employed for the purpose for which the hours are allocated. Three possible arrangements for use of these hours are:

♦ Co-operative teaching where two or more teachers work together with a class. The resource teacher/learning support teacher usually pays particular attention to students with special educational needs or those with low achievement.

♦ Setting the timetable. In this scenario, all students are placed at first in mixed ability classes. Class periods for core subjects (often English, Irish and Maths) are on at the same time. This allows a small group of student with special educational needs or low achievement to receive intensive support in a small class grouping.

♦ Withdrawal of students with individual or small group teaching. Under this arrangement students are withdrawn from mainstream classes for individualised or small group teaching, often in the areas of literacy, maths, or social skills training. A positive feature of this is that it allows a setting where the special needs of a student can be met. A negative effect is the separation of the student from their classmates. The Guidelines state that where there is a withdrawal model in use, that there should be written policy that specifies the circumstances when a student is withdrawn, that mainstream teachers should contribute by advising the resource/learning support teacher about the language, concepts and skills being addressed in the mainstream class. Also when it is proposed to withdraw a student for additional support, the student should be fully involved in planning the intervention, and his/her agreement and the agreement of parents should be obtained. Before the withdrawal programme begins, agreement should be reached on how long the withdrawal intervention should be, dates for a review of the programme, and criteria for the review.

Courses on special needs for teachers and special needs assistants

There has been a huge increase in the provision of resource teaching hours, both full-time and part-time at second-level schools since 2000. This is mirrored in the growth of courses in special educational needs. The website of the Special Education Support Service (www.sess.ie) provides a summary of the courses offered and links to the providers. The list includes:

♦ SESS facilitated courses such as the Annual Conference for Learning Support Teachers.

♦ SESS designed courses such as the course offered to primary and post-primary schools on dyslexia.

♦ On-line courses for teachers on dyslexia, autism, ABA, behaviour management, ADHD and gifted and talented students.

♦ Post graduate diplomas and masters in special educational needs offered by the universities and colleges of education.

♦ Courses for special needs assistants

Students who do not qualify for additional teaching support

These criteria leave a gap in the provision of additional help for many students with dyslexia. Such students, whose intelligence can range from below average through to superior, may not fall within the bottom 10th or 2nd percentile in literacy and numeracy. However they may still experience difficulties at school. The difficulties may include spelling, handwriting, expressing ideas, note-taking or sequencing. As a result of these difficulties they are not achieving their full potential but they do not qualify for additional help in school. In my own school, St. David's, in the school year 2006/2007 there were forty-seven students with diagnosed difficulties ranging from dyslexia to Attention Deficit Disorder (ADD) and Asperger's Syndrome. Approximately twenty-five students were receiving learning support or resource teaching. The other students did not qualify for support and so had to cope for the most part with the effects of their difficulties by themselves or with additional support provided outside school. The DAI workshop classes and exam preparation classes provide an example of the targeted help that can be provided for such students.

REASONABLE ACCOMMODATIONS IN STATE EXAMINATIONS

The report of the Expert Advisory Group on reasonable accommodation in state examinations was published in 2000.

Subsequently circular S11/2000 was issued. The revised arrangements which are relevant to students with dyslexia are:

♦ Applications for reasonable accommodations will now be considered for a student whose intellectual ability is below the average range, but who has a specific learning difficulty.

♦ Up to 2000 there was no indication on the actual certificate or on the statement of results that a student had availed of special arrangements. The circular S11/2000 introduced an explanatory note on the certificate and the statement of results.

♦ The following accommodations are available if appropriate to the needs of the student:
   ✧ Reading Assistance.
   ✧ Tape recorder or computer.
   ✧ Waiver from the spelling and grammatical components in language subjects.

Applications for reasonable accommodation are made by the school. For accommodations in the Leaving Certificate the school sends the application to the Department of Education and Science and includes a psycho-educational assessment report and samples of the student's work. If an application is turned down by the Department of Education and Science, there is an appeals procedure. The members of the group dealing with appeals are drawn from people outside the Department of Education and Science. At Junior Certificate level, the process is simpler.

Approximately 50,000 students sit the Leaving Certificate and Junior Certificate annually, a total of around 100,000 students. The numbers granted reasonable accommodations in 2006 and 2007 are:

	2006 J.C.	2007 J.C	2006 L.C.	2007 L.C.
Use of Tape Recorder	555	580	181	194
Reading Assistance	2769	3101	736	967
Word Processor	138	177	86	135
Spelling/Grammar Waiver	3992	4378	1458	1841

The figures for 2007 are provisional at time of printing. There is a disparity between the numbers for Junior Certificate and the numbers at Leaving Certificate. Possible reasons for this might include:

- Students who do not proceed on to Leaving Certificate.
- A larger cohort of diagnosed students coming through the system.
- Applications for reasonable accommodation at Leaving Certificate level are processed through NEPS. The NEPS psychologist comes to the school to interview the student and staff. In some cases additional testing may be carried out. The psychologist decides if the accommodation is granted. At Junior Certificate level there is a less rigorous application process. The form is simpler and there is no need for an assessment to accompany the application. At this level accommodations are usually granted if the school applies for them.

It is important that there is an objective assessment by the school of which reasonable accommodations, if any, would be appropriate for a particular student. Sometimes parents may be looking for any possible help and yet such help might not be appropriate or helpful to the student. Ways to help determine what accommodations are appropriate can include:

- That teachers mark house examination scripts in language subjects twice, once including the marks for spelling and grammar and then excluding these marks to see if there is a significant difference in overall marks obtained.

- Ask students to prepare for a test on a particular topic. An exam on this material can be given in traditional format and then by using a tape, word processor or a reader. Again the purpose would be to look for a significant difference in marks obtained.

- If the use of a word processor might be appropriate, a preliminary step is the development of excellent keyboarding skills early on at second-level. Otherwise it would not be possible to ascertain if the use of the word processor would be of benefit.

If a particular form of reasonable accommodation is considered appropriate, such accommodation should be given in the house exams in the school. Indeed it is essential that the mock exams prior to the state exam be taken using the accommodation granted. This is very demanding on school resources to provide such accommodations as it may mean that a teacher has to be freed to take such exam students on a one-to-one basis. It may be possible to use parental assistance to help out or to train transition year students to act as readers or supervisors of taping of the exams.

Students will also need training in the use of the accommodation granted. It can be stressful to take an exam aloud with an adult present. Repeated practice can reduce this stress. Students also need to know the role of the supervisor and the help they can give. When reading aloud the supervisor can only read what is on the paper, but students can request particular sections to be reread as frequently as needed. In taping answers, students need practice in giving the exact details such as the number and section of the question they are answering. Answers when taping may be too short, possibly because they cannot check what they have already answered easily, whereas with a written answer, it is possible to quickly scan the answer above. Students could use some blank paper to help structure answers by making a list of the points they are going to include before speaking to the tape. This will help with fluency. They must also make sure only to press the 'Record' button when speaking otherwise the tape is very lengthy with long silences. Another reason for short answers might be because of embarrassment in the one-to-one situation with the supervisor. The school appoints the supervisor for state examinations which are taken with a reader or by tape and it is possible that it can be someone with whom the student is familiar. This can reduce the embarrassment.

In the case of the reasonable accommodations of reading assistance, use of a tape or word processor, students are in an exam centre by themselves. The fact that students are separated from the rest of the student body during the exams is a very public statement. This is at a time of development in adolescence when many young people want to be part of the peer group and do not want to be considered different. As a result some students opt not to use the accommodation even if granted. However they should consider the real benefits in terms of the results before making a quick decision and opting out of using the accommodation.

The introduction of the explanatory note on the certificate is a cause of concern to the Dyslexia Association and to parents. It is a permanent statement on the certificate of the student. For future employers, who may not be familiar with dyslexia and its effects, the wording of the different explanatory notes might imply the student cannot read, or spell or use grammar at all. This is more important to the student who opts for employment after second-level. There is no such explanatory note on the certificates, diplomas and degrees issued by third-level colleges, and employers in all probability will not ask to see the Junior or Leaving Certificates of applicants with such higher qualifications.

In 2006 a case was taken by two Leaving certificate students to the Equality Tribunal. The Tribunal found that the Department of Education and Science had discriminated against the two students by annotating their results. The Department were instructed to issue new certificates without annotation and to pay €6,000 to each student. The Department appealed the decision and the case was heard in July 2007. At the time of going to press the result is expected in October 2007. In the meantime, the Department continues to annotate certificates.

Many parents, worried about the explanatory note, would prefer not to apply for accommodations if the student can cope at all with the traditional format of the exam. Therefore when deciding whether to apply for the exemption from spelling and grammar elements of the exam, a key factor may be the amount of marks allocated for spelling and grammar. For example, if the allocated marks are 10% or less, a parent might consider the student could cope without the exemption and pass the exam, whereas if the allocated marks were more than this percentage, it could lead to the student failing the exam. However for students applying to CAO, the extra marks gained through reasonable accommodations mean their points score could increase as a result of a change of grade. To go from a 'C2' to a 'C1' results in an additional five points. For these reasons it is important for parents to know the marks allocated for spelling and grammar. The Chief Examiner in English states the marks allocated for spelling and grammar are as follows:

♦ At Junior Certificate, higher level, 15 marks out of 70 are allocated for spelling and grammar in the personal writing section and 7 out of 30 are allocated in the functional writing section. Elsewhere throughout the papers at higher, ordinary and foundation levels, answers are marked by impression, with spelling and grammar forming an integral part of that impression.

♦ For English at Leaving Certificate, higher and ordinary levels, 10% of the marks will be allocated to spelling and grammar in Papers 1 and 2.

Marking schemes in the other language subjects are available from the State Examinations Commission and are published on the website www.examinations.ie.

The examiners of scripts in the state examinations are second-level teachers. Many teachers have not received formal training in how dyslexia presents in written work in either pre-service or in-service training. As a result they may not be aware of how bizarre the phonic spelling of some students with dyslexia can be. Examples of phonic spelling from students' work include the following:

♦ amjedidly for immediately.

♦ anctus for anxious.

♦ enchivative for initiative.

♦ aricaligest for archaeologist.

♦ barax for barracks.

The examiner might have to read such scripts out aloud in order to perceive the word the student means. Correcting exam papers for students with dyslexia takes more time. Poor handwriting, bizarre spellings and poorly expressed facts can mean the teacher has to decipher the script to see if the student has the correct answers. One example of this is where a student lost six marks in the mock Science examination at Junior Certificate for saying that a bimetallic strip 'would bend' under heat. However he spelt 'bend' with six letters (bouend) and it was marked as an incorrect answer. If examiners do not have experience of dyslexic scripts, it is quite possible that they might consider answers spelt bizarrely as wrong and not refer the script to more experienced examiners. Such a concern is noted in the Report of the Task Force on Dyslexia. In the past the special arrangement whereby an examiner was informed of the individual student's difficulties meant the script of the student with dyslexia was flagged. This would alert them to such difficulties. Now such notification is not given and there is no flagging of these scripts. I believe that until the time all in the teaching profession have received training on the topic of dyslexia and other learning difficulties, examiners should receive training in how dyslexia presents in scripts. This could form part of the correcting conferences which are held in June when the examiners receive guidelines on the correction of scripts.

REASONABLE ACCOMMODATION IN HOUSE AND MOCK EXAMINATIONS

If students are entitled to reasonable accommodation in state exams, it is only fair that such accommodation also be given in the house exams. This should be part of school policy on dyslexia. Teachers should be reminded of the student's difficulties prior to the exams and, if appropriate, arrangements made for them to take the exams by tape or on word processor, have the papers read to them or have an exemption from the spelling and grammar elements of the language subjects.

An example of the benefits of accommodations in house examinations comes from my own school. A student entered second-level who had been diagnosed as having dyslexia. He had attended St. Oliver Plunkett's Reading School in Monkstown. He had received remedial help and had good family support. He was co-operative and pleasant and always did his homework. At Christmas in 1st year he took History as one of his first exams. He got 8%. The teacher was unhappy to give him such a poor mark. He had worked hard during the term and had seemed to understand what was being taught. She was worried that his self-confidence would be badly affected by such a low mark. It was decided to read the exam paper to him and write down his answers. His marks went from 8% to 55%. He had got similarly poor marks in Geography and Science. His teachers gave the tests orally and his grades in Science went from 12% to 54%. In Geography his grades went from 11% to 44%. If the history teacher had not raised the issue of his grade, he would have failed his Christmas tests badly. As it was, he did quite well. Also the school would not have become aware of the huge discrepancy between his written and oral performances. Below are examples of his answers on the written test and his answers from the oral test.

Geography short questions	His written answer	His answer after the question was read to him and his answer written down
Magma is	volcanic metel	molten material inside the earth core
Three things that happen at the plate margins are	earthqua volceno	earthquakes volcanoes geysers
The three rock types are	ignus metamorphic	metamorphic igneous sedimentary
Three uses of limestone are		making churches making fireplaces
A slag heap is		dust from a coal mine
Weathering is		rain falls on rock, and wears the rock away
A permeable rock is a rock which		water gets through

His lack of ability to read accurately and quickly and to express his knowledge in written form were major impediments to his passing written exams, yet he had the knowledge if he was examined orally. In his case the school requested a reader and the facility to tape his answers in state examinations. He passed all his examinations at Junior Certificate and obtained four honours grades on higher papers.

If mock papers are sent outside the school for correction, a note should be attached to the paper explaining that the student is receiving reasonable accommodations in the state exams. An incident which illustrates the importance of such communication is the case of a student with dyslexia who sat a Junior Certificate higher level English mock paper. The paper was returned with the comment that the spelling was so disgraceful that higher level English was out of the question. This had a negative effect on the student's confidence when sitting the actual exam in the Junior Certificate.

COMMUNICATION AMONG THE STAFF

In another incident the student, whose geography test is quoted above, also provided an example of how important it is that all relevant school staff be informed of a student's difficulty. The student had a detention. The Year Head, who was supervising the detention, was not aware of his learning difficulties and handed out the usual detention work. The student was not able to do it. At the end of the detention period he was given another detention because he had not done the required work. It was sorted out later but he was very upset, as was the Year Head when informed of the student's reasons for not completing the assignment.

A communications system should be set up which will routinely inform the staff of a particular student's difficulties. This could include giving a profile of the student's strengths and weaknesses and suggestions about effective teaching and testing strategies. Such information is highly confidential. If it is given in written form it is advisable to give the information on these students identifying each student by number only and handing out a separate index. The Task Force Report states that mainstream teachers should assume major responsibility for the progress and development of each student in their classes who has learning difficulties arising from dyslexia, with learning support and resource teachers and other professionals assuming supporting roles. They need information on students to be able to do this.

PHOTOCOPYING NOTES AND USE OF REVISION BOOKS

All students can benefit greatly from good notes. It is more beneficial that students summarise their textbooks themselves as it helps them structure and absorb the information. However it is likely that students with dyslexia will find it difficult to summarise material in books and make their own notes. This can be due to poor or slow reading where they may have to reread a piece several times to see the points the writer is making, difficulties in summarising and organising material or difficulties in making legible and clearly laid-out notes. The essential task is to learn the information. Having to make their own notes from the text can place additional barriers in their way.

These students can therefore benefit hugely from getting precise and concise notes. The source of such notes could be teacher notes or copies of the notes of other students. Good notes give them the tools to learn. Some students with dyslexia have difficulty seeing and organising patterns. Good notes are an effective way for them to see the structure of what they are learning. The notes are a useful device in organising material and are helpful in formatting their own answers. Because the notes are structured, the student can use that structure when answering questions. Revision handbooks are of use if students are not provided with photocopied notes.

If teachers dictate their own notes to the class, it can be a problem for students with dyslexia. Some students have a difficulty in visualising the words being called. They have to think about the shape of the words and then they have lost the next point the teacher makes. If necessary, the teacher should arrange for photocopies of notes to be given to the student. These could be photocopies of the teacher's own notes or a photocopy of the notes of a student who takes well-organised, legible notes.

Here is an excerpt from an essay a sixteen year old girl wrote about her dyslexia.

'My head ached, letters churned in my mind. I wanted to scream. I glanced at my friend's masterpiece, every word spelt correctly and a page of beautiful writing, the work teachers love. Slowly I looked at my own copy, half finished sentences, words spelt incorrectly. I placed my hand over my work, embarrassed in case any one would see it. As the Junior Certificate approached and more notes were being called out, the more lost I became. Each time a word was spelt out to me, it became more jumbled. I got so frustrated. I wanted to give up. I would go out with my friends, when deep down I knew I should be studying. But there seemed little point. I would study and make notes, but I seemed to remember very little. I know that something was wrong, but did not know what. Finally it dawned on me. Maybe I had a learning problem. I could not explain but I had a funny feeling it was dyslexia. I did not know much about it. My parents were very supportive. I was diagnosed as having dyslexia. In a way I felt relieved to know I had dyslexia and that I was not thick. I felt angry and confused and wished I did not have it. What angered me most was finding out two weeks before my Junior Certificate, as I worried I would not be able to spell words in the exam.'

She was a student who had gone through primary school without being identified as having dyslexia. When she did her entrance test, her scores were in the average range. There were no perceived weaknesses on her profile of ability. The use of the Dyslexia Screening Test or LASS Secondary may have helped to identify her difficulties earlier, but they were not available at the time. During her first three years in the school she worked very hard but was always disappointed at her results. She felt it took her much longer than others to absorb written material. She had to reread articles many times to make sense of them. She was spending longer hours on homework than the school would recommend. Prior to her Junior Certificate, the frustration of trying to take notes overwhelmed her. She could not visualise what she was to write when the teacher called out notes. She had developed coping mechanisms such as copying from a friend or waiting for others to ask the teacher to repeat a phrase. If the teacher spelt something out, she virtually had to translate the spelling into what the word looked like. If the teacher, when spelling out a word, said 'double O', she would have to ask herself 'what does that look like?' She spoke to her parents saying that she thought she was dyslexic. Her assessment showed this was the case. Because she had worked hard and had learnt to read at the expected ages, she had gone undiagnosed until this stage.

Have a look at the notes in Fig.8.1 and ask which notes could you learn from best.

(A)

Implications of the Companies Act 1980

1. If a company has engaged in reckless trading, a director may become a restricted director. He may not be able to take part in a company for five years and loses limited liability.

2. A director involved in fraud or dishonesty may be disqualified for a stipulated period.

(B)

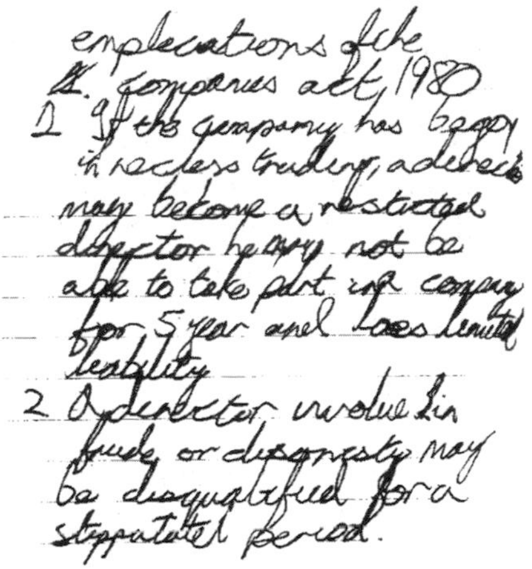

[handwritten notes]

(C)

emplications of the companies act 1980
1. If the company has begoy in recless trading, a director may become a restricted director he may not be able to take part in a company for 5 year and loes limited liability
2. A director involve in frude or disonesty may be disqualified for a stipputated period.

Fig. 8.1 (A) shows typewritten Business Organisation Notes which were dictated. (B) shows the notes taken by a student with dyslexia (C) shows the typed written version of the student's notes

A school policy that would allow the photocopying of notes is of benefit to students with dyslexia.

TAPES

Tapes of notes or texts can help some students with dyslexia to learn. This might be apparent in the psychological report where good auditory memory is commented on. The material is being presented through two senses, sight and hearing. Teachers could suggest to parents or to students themselves that notes be taped, in order to see if this is beneficial.

In some subjects, in particular English, videos and tapes of texts are commercially available. If reading is laboured, students can lose the thread of the story because it is such hard work to decipher the text. Listening to a tape of a novel while they read it can mean they may become engrossed in the story. They do not have to look up difficult words as they hear them. They can get familiar with characters and plots. If the poems are taped, it can help them to become familiar with them. DVDs of Shakespearean plays allow the play come alive and make it easier to write about. It does not replace reading the play which needs to be done for students' own reading development and to make them familiar with the spelling of names but it helps their knowledge of the text.

In Junior Certificate English, the teacher has great freedom to choose texts. It makes sense that if there is a student with dyslexia in the class that the teacher would choose textbooks that are available on tape.

If the students are not readers, the teacher could encourage them to widen their knowledge of literature by using tapes of books. For some students reading does not become any easier. They may have good functional reading skills but reading will never become a pleasurable activity. Part of their coping mechanism is to look for alternative ways to get information and be up-to-date with current books. Tapes, radio and television can provide other routes to information.

ALTERNATIVE FORMATS

There have been major developments in the provision of alternative formats for learning materials. Dolphin Publishers www.yourdolphin.com have developed tools to allow people with dyslexia or a visual impairment to access learning materials in alternative formats such as MP3, DAISY digital talking books, Braille and large print. The software allows teachers quickly convert any Word document into a DAISY digital talking book. As the file is read aloud, the corresponding words are highlighted for the student to follow on the screen. It can be burned on to CD, copied directly to a MP3 player or simply made available for students to download.

In 2007 the Dyslexia Association of Ireland, AHEAD and the National Council for the Blind were involved in a pilot project on use of alternative formats for printed material. A Leaving Certificate Geography text book was put onto DAISY format and students were given the CD and CD player. They were able to use the CD on the computer where all the maps and illustrations were available while the text was read aloud. The CD differed from the usual talking book as it corresponded exactly to the text and students were able to pinpoint a particular chapter, page or heading immediately. It is hoped to persuade educational publishers to make disks available with text books, either included in the price which would be a little higher for every book or to purchased separately with a copy of the text.

Screening and Identification of Pupils with Dyslexia

Up to 1996 there has been no screening test for dyslexia, either at primary school level or at second-level. Psychological assessment was suggested by teachers if the child failed to achieve in reading and writing by the age of eight or nine. So, while it is likely that severely affected students would be identified, borderline students who achieved reading could slip through the net. Dr. B. Hornsby in her book *Overcoming Dyslexia* calls these students 'hidden dyslexics' and suggests it is only when their earlier promise is not fulfilled in exams that teachers and parents begin to ask questions.

Since the early 90's, over seventy students have been diagnosed as having dyslexia or other learning difficulties in my own school. All had gone through primary school without being identified or sent for assessment. Two students were identified from the Differential Aptitude Testing done in third year. One of these students had a percentile score of seventy-five in abstract reasoning and two in verbal reasoning. One student, out of frustration, had raised the question herself because of her difficulties in taking notes. Other students were identified from the entrance assessment where an uneven pattern of ability might raise questions. LASS Secondary is now being used in the school to help identify students with difficulties. In all cases a full psycho-educational assessment needs to be carried out in order to make a diagnosis.

New screening tests became available in 1996. Particularly important are the tests for the younger age group. It is important that students with dyslexia are identified in their early years at primary level before they start to fail and their self-esteem suffers.

The DST (Dyslexia Screening Test) is now available to help screen students in the age-group 6 years and 6 months to 16 years and 5 months. It could be used if a teacher has any suspicion that a student may have dyslexia. A second screening instrument is LASS Secondary. This is a computer aided screening test available since 2000. Such screening instruments should be available in all schools.

It is important that teachers be aware of inconsistencies and behaviour that might indicate dyslexia. The report of the Task Force on Dyslexia set out four different age-related checklists of indicators of a possible learning difficulty. The appropriate checklist for post-primary students (12+ years) is given below.

- ♦ When looking at the lists of indicators, remember the following:
- ♦ No child will have all the indicators.
- ♦ Many children will have several of the indicators.
- ♦ Some indicators are more common than others.
- ♦ The number of indicators observed in a child does not indicate whether the child's dyslexia is mild, moderate or severe.

Indicators of a possible learning difficulty arising from dyslexia (ages 12 Years+)

- ♦ Is still reading slowly and without fluency, with many inaccuracies.
- ♦ Misreads words (e.g. *hysterical* for *historical*) or information.
- ♦ Has difficulty modifying reading rate.
- ♦ Has an inadequate store of knowledge due to lack of reading experience.
- ♦ Continues to experience serious spelling difficulties.
- ♦ Has slow, dysfluent and/or illegible handwriting.
- ♦ Has better oral skills than written skills.

Has difficulty planning, sequencing and organising written text.

Has difficulty with written syntax or punctuation.

Has difficulty skimming, scanning and/or proof reading written text.

♦ Has trouble summarising or outlining.

♦ Has problems in taking notes and copying from the board.

♦ Procrastinates and/or avoids reading and writing tasks.

♦ Does not complete assignments or class work or does not hand them in.

♦ Is slow in answering questions, especially open-ended ones.

Has poor memorisation skills.

♦ Still mispronounces or misuses some words.

♦ Has problems recalling the names of some words or objects.

Has poor planning and organisation skills.

♦ Has poor time management skills.

Has more difficulty in language-based subjects (e.g. English, Irish, History) than in non-language based subjects (e.g. Mathematics, Technical Graphics).

Lacks self-confidence and has poor self-image.

A combination of several of these indicators should lead teachers to question whether there is a specific learning difficulty present. The use of DST or LASS Secondary may help confirm suspicions. The teacher should then consult with the student's parents. It is only with a psycho-educational assessment that a diagnosis of dyslexia can be made. The development of NEPS should help in accessing assessments but NEPS is not fully staffed yet. When parents pay for the assessment, the cost can be claimed as an expense for income tax purposes.

READABILITY OF TEXTBOOKS

Readability of textbooks is a key issue. Some Junior Certificate books span the total course of three years and are written with the third year student who may be fifteen years old in mind. Such textbooks provide a reading challenge to students in first year who may be twelve years old and in particular to the student whose reading age is below that of their peers due to dyslexia or other reasons.

An analysis of commonly-used textbooks for the Junior Certificate using the Flesch-Kincaid Grade Level Readability Test showed that the average first year student would have difficulty in reading and comprehending the contents of some of these texts. The Flesch-Kincaid Test had been used as a U.S. Government standard because many Government agencies require documents and forms to meet specific readability levels. One of the main uses of the test is in Education. The Flesch-Kincaid Grade Level Formula makes it possible for teachers, parents, librarians and others to judge the readability level of books and texts. It provides a grade level for a text. This grade level can be equated with a reading age. The Formula is:

$$0.39 \left(\frac{\text{total words}}{\text{total sentences}} \right) + 11.8 \left(\frac{\text{total syllables}}{\text{total words}} \right) - 15.59$$

On the basis of this test, while some textbooks come out with a reading age equivalent of twelve, a commonly used Junior Certificate Home Economics book had a reading age equivalent of fifteen and similarly a commonly-used Junior Certificate Religion book had a reading age equivalent of sixteen. Such texts pose enormous access difficulties for average students, and even more for the student with dyslexia or poor reading skills in general.

Readability should be a key factor in deciding on textbooks so that the material is accessible to students.

STANDARDISED TESTS

Standardised tests are tests given under very strict conditions. The purpose of the test is to give a result which shows how a student achieved in relation to the population of students of the same age and sex. This is done by comparing the result to norms that have been researched. Such standardised tests include the Micra T tests, Drumcondra Tests, Differential Aptitude Tests (DATS), AH2 and AH4.

For some of these tests timing is critical. Students are not meant to finish the test in the time allocated. The score is derived from how far they get through the test in the time allotted. In other tests the time is not so important. The allotted time is so generous that the vast majority of students will have answered all the questions with plenty of time to spare.

It may be difficult to get an accurate result on such tests for the student with dyslexia for the following reasons:

♦ The student may be slower in processing information. Here is an example based on the DATS (Differential Aptitude Testing). There is a generous time allowance for completing all but one section of the DATS. The vast majority of students finish the questions well within the time allotted. A student with dyslexia in my own school did the Numerical Reasoning section. The student completed twenty-seven out of the forty questions consecutively and then ran out of time. All of his answers to that point were correct. It was obvious that with more time this student would have completed more questions and obtained a higher score. His result is different to the student who has completed the full forty questions within the allotted time and got thirteen incorrect. Yet both students would be given the same result.

♦ The student may be slower in reading the instructions or in deciphering the sequence of instructions. They may lack the vocabulary to be able to do the task required. This is critically important in Maths testing. Here is an example of a Maths question from a standardised test.

John spends three times as much as Michael on bus fares each week and Michael spends three times as much as Martin. If John spends 45p, how much does Martin spend?

For some students with dyslexia such a question is more a test of their English skills than their Maths abilities. They may need time to work out the words mean and to interpret the sequence of instructions correctly. This makes their work much slower and sometimes they may not successfully decode what it is they are meant to do.

An example from another standardised test is as follows. It is a test of the student's ability to classify. They have to underline the odd one out from a series of words such as the following: *Butcher, vicar, grocer, baker*. The students are given forty such problems and a limited amount of time in which to answer. No student is expected to complete the entire test. The score is based on how far they progress in the test. Lack of vocabulary and slowness in reading the words on the page can slow down their answering. It is the processing of information and their reading skills that affect their scores.

It is important that parents, students, and teachers realise the limitations and unreliability of these tests for students with dyslexia and other learning difficulties. **They are not valid predictors of the student's ability**. Such students are likely to have a far more valid instrument of their ability in the psycho-educational assessment.

At primary level, no critical decisions are made based on standardised tests. However the results could affect the child's self image. Despite being told not to, students do compare the results achieved. Therefore it is important that the child understands the results are not reliable. Also, if a teacher has not received training on the topic of learning difficulties, he/she also might form expectations of the child based on the results of standardised testing. This is why it is so important that the psycho-educational assessment is brought into school and the student's profile with its strengths and weaknesses is discussed with the teacher.

Far more important is the fact that these tests may be used at entrance assessment at second-level. Crucial decisions may be based on the student's performance in this assessment such as class placement.

The Post-primary Guidelines on Inclusion of Students with Special Educational Needs state: 'Standardised tests are often unsuitable for use with students with special educational needs, because the language register inherent in many tests makes them inaccessible to this population. Therefore caution should be exercised in using and interpreting the results of these tests.'

The Civil Service Commission allows students with dyslexia additional time when taking standardised testing for recruitment purposes.

Extra Curricular Activities

Most writers on dyslexia describe the effect it has on self-esteem and confidence. Students have experienced failure from a very early age in a key part of life, that of academic achievement. It is also a very public arena since all students in a classroom know the student who has difficulties in achieving. This failure in academic achievement can ripple through many aspects of life affecting relationships with peers, leading to a lack of confidence that may lead them into not trusting their abilities and being unwilling to try or join in new experiences. The lack of confidence may be worse if the dyslexia is not diagnosed until second-level.

Some students may find an escape mechanism from being thought 'stupid and thick' by avoiding school work and by confronting authority. It is more acceptable among the student's peers that poor grades are the result of being a 'tough' man rather than the result of a learning difficulty. Others have become expert in evading work. Since many teachers have not been trained to recognise and deal with dyslexia, these students can get away with these avoidance tactics. This highlights the need for teacher training.

As part of school policy, some brief description of dyslexia and how it affects students should be given perhaps in the pastoral care programme or the study skills programme. It makes it easier for students to be open about difficulties when other students understand about dyslexia. They may also realise that other students can also be affected and that they are not alone.

Students with dyslexia are likely to experience failure to some extent in their academic studies. If self-esteem and confidence are to be developed it will be in other aspects of life. It is really important that these students get involved in activities where they can achieve and be part of the wider school community. Sometimes, because of their low self-esteem, they may be reluctant to join in extra-curricular activities and may need active encouragement from parents and school staff. Types of activities may include all types of sports, clubs, drama, voluntary work and projects. Part of the support service the school should offer is active intervention in encouraging these students to become involved in such activities.

School Structures

Below are some suggestions on possible support services for students with dyslexia.

♦ If students have exceptionally weak reading and writing skills, is there an assessment to check if there is a significant difference in their exam performance if they take an exam orally with a reader or with a taping facility? This would be to check if it would be appropriate to apply for such facilities in State exams.

♦ If reasonable accommodation is given for state exams, is it available for house exams?

♦ If verbal skills are so poor that students might have difficulty understanding the format of questions in the entrance assessment, does the school make a reader or other assistance available to them? Whereas a reading test will give an accurate picture of reading skills, a Maths test, where students do not understand what is being asked because of the language content or sequencing of the questions, does not measure Maths ability.

♦ If there is streaming, does it take account of the student with dyslexia who may be very intelligent and articulate but who has some verbal difficulties?

♦ If places in a particular option are limited, would the school consider giving positive discrimination to such students when allocating places?

♦ If a student has excellent Maths but poor language skills, will the student be able to do Higher Level Maths?

♦ If Irish is part of the entrance assessment and the student has an exemption from Irish, is there a mechanism to take this into account in the overall placement?

♦ If the student is exempt from Irish, is it possible to arrange for another subject or activity to be done during this free time?

♦ Is a third language obligatory in the option structure?

♦ Are students with learning difficulties given training in study skills?

♦ Do students have access to computers? Can extra computer time be made available so students can develop good keyboard skills? If this cannot be done in school time, can it be arranged after school? Parents may be willing to pay for this.

♦ Have teachers received in-service training on dyslexia and other learning difficulties?

♦ Are mainstream teachers reminded on a regular basis of the difficulties of these students?

HELP WITH THE TRANSITION TO SECOND-LEVEL

The transition to second-level may be daunting to the student with low self-esteem or with social difficulties. The second-level school is much larger both in size and in number of teachers and pupils. Possibly the student may not know any one else going to the school, so the first day is a major hurdle. A school in south Dublin has introduced a scheme to help these students cope. Parents are informed of the scheme and if they think it appropriate, such students are invited to attend the school for an orientation day. This is held the day before the term commences. They are introduced to the other students in the group, teachers, the layout of the school and the timetable. Part of the day includes games and quizzes on what they have learnt. On the following day, when the school opens for all incoming first years, these students have the edge. They can take the lead and show the other students around and can introduce teachers. They also know the other members of the group so they are not alone.

DYSLEXIA FRIENDLY SCHOOLS

The dyslexia friendly school is a concept pioneered by the British Dyslexia Association (BDA) and has been embraced by many schools and Local Education Authorities (LEAs) throughout the UK and in the USA. A BDA Quality Mark has been introduced which promotes inclusion through dyslexia friendly LEAs and schools. Progress is being made to introduce the concept in Northern Ireland. The initiative aims to identify, promote and celebrate excellent practice in improving access to learning for children. Part of the reason it has been so successful are the changes that make schools more dyslexia friendly also lead to more effective schools for all students.

The British Dyslexia Association has published a resource pack *Achieving Dyslexia Friendly Schools*. It is available on their website: www.bdadyslexia.org.uk. It states that LEAs are beginning to report improvements in key indicators of effectiveness such as:

Attendance.

Performance in examinations.

Pupil confidence, self-esteem and behaviour.

Parental confidence.

Teacher confidence following whole-school training.

LEAs are also beginning to report reductions in exclusions and appeals.

The concept of dyslexia friendly means that the school culture would include some of the following characteristics:

Gardner's Theory of Multiple Intelligences which outlines that there are at least seven intelligences, each with its own preferred way of learning. Everyone possesses varying degrees of each of these intelligences. Teachers, who ensure that class instruction is structured to use the different learning preferences of students, empower more students to be successful in their learning.

Supportive environment where the learner feels safe and supported and where teachers make it transparently clear that it is OK to be dyslexic.

Clear guidelines about tasks, what is to be achieved and how it will be assessed with positive feedback from teachers including constructive comments on how improvements can be made.

♦ Setting achievable goals is crucial to the self-esteem of the student.

Empowering students by allowing them discuss what helps and what does not help.

Teacher self-evaluation.

How Subject Teachers Can Help

9

At second-level while there is continuing development of numeracy and literacy skills, there are new challenges to be faced. If students are to succeed in examinations they must be able to access subject content and then to communicate the knowledge learnt. Learning support and resource teachers have an input on the development of literacy and numeracy skills if the student falls within the criteria for such help. However many students with dyslexia do not fall within such criteria. However all students with dyslexia, whether they receive extra help or not, rely on the mainstream teacher for subject teaching. This means each teacher needs to understand how dyslexia affects students and the most appropriate teaching strategies and supports for students to help them reach their full potential.

The Task Force on Dyslexia recognised the key involvement of mainstream teachers both in identifying possible learning difficulties arising from dyslexia and in addressing the needs of students identified as having such difficulties. It states that mainstream teachers should assume major responsibility for the progress and development of each student in their classes who has learning difficulties arising from dyslexia, with learning support and resource teachers and other professionals assuming supporting roles. The Task Force recommended that subject teachers "provide differentiated instruction" to such students.

Differentiation is the process where teachers select appropriate teaching methods to match an individual student's learning strategies within the class group. The Department of Education and Science Inspectorate look for differentiation during subject inspections. There are many ways it can be done. Here are some examples:

♦ If the student has strong visual spatial ability, videos, tapes, drawings, diagrams or mindmaps could be used to present information, both by the teacher when teaching and the student when doing homework.

♦ Use multi-sensory teaching methods so that as many as possible of the student's senses are being stimulated.

♦ Adapt class and homework goals for individual students. For a student with writing difficulties, accept answers which are shorter than the class average as it may take this student longer to produce the short answer.

The fact that many second-level subject teachers are not aware of the needs of these students is not surprising when one considers that there has been little or no input on dyslexia and other learning difficulties during the pre-service training courses in the past. Even now few teachers have done in-career training on the topic. The Task Force on Dyslexia made eight recommendations on teacher training, including the recommendation that pre-service courses at primary and post-primary levels should include input on Special Needs Education, both integrated within general courses and as an area of study itself. Attention should also be given to ways in which the class and subject teachers can identify and meet the needs of students with learning difficulties arising from dyslexia.

At second-level there is a defined amount of knowledge to be conveyed during a class period and often the underlying assumption is that every child absorbs information from the teacher in the same way. Consider that at second-level a teacher may teach close to two hundred students in a week. Taking the conservative estimate of an incidence rate of 4% of dyslexia in the general population, this means that up to eight of those students could be affected. Dyslexia is not like a physical disability where the student can still learn through the normal classroom techniques. It affects the entire dynamic between pupil and teacher. Teaching is about communicating information. Dyslexia affects communication. The teacher may think he/she has effectively given information to the student but this may not be the case. If the teacher is not aware of the symptoms and effects of dyslexia, the student may be classified as careless, lazy or stubborn.

An understanding of dyslexia by the teaching profession would minimise such problems.

This point is illustrated by a survey of the second-level students who attended the DAI AGM in 2005. Forty students completed the questionnaire. The findings include the following:

- 45% of the students had to look after their own needs such as getting notes, organising a reader for examinations or placing a desk near a power point for a laptop. A further 30% had to do this sometimes.

- In 25% of the schools represented by the students, it was the school who took the responsibility to inform the teachers of the student's difficulties. Otherwise it was the parents or students themselves who had to inform teachers.

- 47.5% of the students felt teachers need to get informed about dyslexia. Overall students felt teachers did not understand dyslexia and the difficulties students experience in the classroom. One student made the comment that older teachers did not care but that the younger teachers helped and cared more.

A key factor which would improve the situation is the provision of teacher training, both in-career and pre-service. Second-level schools are entitled to one day's in-service training for the whole staff once a year. Using this day to give the whole staff information on dyslexia and other learning difficulties would be an immediate and effective way to provide such training. The Special Education Support Service provides such training.

Sources of Information about Dyslexia for Teachers

These include:

- The video/CD ROM/DVD *Understanding Dyslexia* is a joint initiative of the Departments of Education in Ireland, North and South. It was issued to all schools in 2005. This is an invaluable source of information and includes sections on the psychological assessment, teaching strategies at primary and post-primary and advice for parents. The resources section on the CD ROM/DVD includes extensive and comprehensive information on books, tests, ICT material and websites. Highlighted in the section for post-primary teachers is the following definition of fairness.

'To successfully manage the inclusive classroom, teachers should re-examine the notion of what is 'fair'. 'Fair' does not mean every pupil gets the same treatment but that every pupil gets what he or she needs. Equity should be promoted in every classroom'.

◆ The psycho-educational assessment may include a profile of the student's learning strengths and needs as well as practical suggestions about appropriate teaching strategies. If teachers have difficulty understanding the terminology used in the assessment, the CD ROM provides a guide to its interpretation.

◆ Students and parents are also a source of information about techniques that work or do not work. Parents may have been involved from an early age in providing support for homework and may be very familiar with the student's difficulties.

◆ The CD ROM *Understanding Dyslexia* has a self-help questionnaire for the student. The purpose of this is to help students analyse how they learn and how teachers could help. Asking the student such questions can be a very effective part of an evaluation of teaching strategies by the teacher.

◆ *Inclusion of Students with Special Educational Needs: Post Primary Guidelines*. These guidelines were published in 2007 and sets out advice and a best practice model for school managements and teachers in relation to the education of students with special educational needs. Section 5 concentrates on teaching and learning in the inclusive classroom. Strategies and approaches that are effective in the teaching and learning of students with special educational needs are discussed. These strategies can also be effectively used with all students in the class.

◆ *Guidelines for Teachers of Students with General Learning Difficulties*. These guidelines, issued in 2007 on a CD, are aimed at teachers of students with mild, moderate and severe learning difficulties at primary level and students of mild learning difficulties at post-primary. The guidelines have been circulated to all schools. They identify potential areas of difficulty, their implications for learning and possible teaching strategies. They include suggested methodologies, exemplars of approach and worksheets. At post-primary level, there are comprehensive and very practical sections for teachers of most post-primary subjects including Art, Business Studies, CSPE, Drama, English, Gaeilge, Geography, History, Home Economics, Music, Physical Education, Religion, Science, SPHE and Technology.

♦ Each school should have a communication process so that every mainstream teacher is informed of a student's profile, highlighting the strengths and needs. This should be done in September of each school year and at regular intervals during the year. Information on which students are availing of accommodations in examinations should be passed on.

♦ Under the Education of Persons with Special Educational Needs Act 2004 there is an obligation that individual education plans (IEPs) are in place for students with special needs. Under the Learning Support Guidelines 2000, individual profile and pupil learning programmes (IPLPs) should be prepared for students qualifying for learning support teaching. It is recommended that these plans and programmes are drawn up on a whole-school approach involving mainstream teachers, the learning support and resource teacher, the parents and the pupil themselves.

♦ Each school should build up a library of relevant texts for teachers. There are an increasing number of books becoming available on practical strategies for teachers in different subjects areas at second-level. The book *Dyslexia – Successful Inclusion in the Secondary School* by Peer and Reid has chapters dedicated to teaching in subject areas such as Physics, Biology, Maths, History, Geography, Art and Music, English and foreign languages. Again, the CD ROM *Understanding Dyslexia* has extensive list of resources and books. The British Dyslexia Association has a series of books on teaching different subjects at second-level.

POSSIBLE TEACHING STRATEGIES

Some of the topics in the previous chapter would be relevant to the subject teacher such as note-taking, alternative formats and taping. However there are specific techniques that the subject teacher can use in the classroom that will help the student with dyslexia. I appreciate how difficult some of these may be to implement for a busy class teacher. At second-level a teacher might easily deal with two hundred students in a single day and has classroom contact with a particular class for approximately three hours in a week. The Task Force on Dyslexia recommended that subject teachers 'provide differentiated instruction to students who have learning difficulties arising from dyslexia'. To tailor teaching techniques to meet individual needs takes time and time is at a premium. However some of these students will fail unless teachers are aware of their specific difficulties and try to find some teaching methods that will help them to achieve. Here are ideas that may help:

- ♦ The student may have great difficulty in deciphering script handwriting whether it is on the board, in notes or on exam papers. Teacher notes and test papers should be typed. It is recommended that type should be clear and well separated, using a minimum font size of 12 or 14. Sans serif fonts are best, e.g. Arial, Comic Sans, Verdana, Helvetica, and Tahoma. Use lower case or sentence case, as using all capitals can make it harder to read.

- ♦ Break down a series of instructions into simple commands. Do not give an instruction which is a complicated sequence, e.g. 'After you have taken down your homework and before you leave the room, clean the desk'. Break it down to a series of simpler commands, 'Take down your homework', 'Clean your desk', 'Now you can leave'. The student, who has difficulty with sequences or who has to decipher what is being said, gets confused unless instructions are kept simple.

- ♦ Some students with dyslexia have difficulty remembering sequences such as days of the week or months of the year and this can lead to conflict with adult demands. A student may have been given homework as follows: an essay for Monday,

Maths for Tuesday, revision of a text in Geography for next Thursday and reading for a book report to be handed up in two weeks time. Teachers assume that the student will see time and sequence clearly in much the same way as they do. However, because of sequencing difficulties, there may be confusion about the instructions. The student then gets into trouble with teachers for not having work done. It is easy for adults to conclude that such students are lazy or careless. To overcome this, ensure they use a homework notebook properly with a system that will remind them of tasks.

♦ Give them plenty of time to write in homework as they can be much slower than other students in taking information down.

♦ Give written notices of events. Most second-level students are more than capable of listening and taking home clear details. However it is very likely that students with learning difficulties will neglect to take home a key fact or they will get the facts confused.

♦ Some students will understand the sequence of steps in a Maths problem, a Science experiment or a book-keeping problem in class and appear to be competent but will have difficulty remembering the sequence later due to short term memory difficulties. Whereas the average student might need to do an example four or five times to be sure of the sequence of steps, some students with learning difficulties may need to over-learn the sequence by doing more examples.

♦ Some students may not decode what it is they are being asked to do in a question. It is important that they are taught how questions are structured and what are the precise meanings of words used in questions. The student may misinterpret the small link words and yet these radically affect the meaning of a question.

♦ Check if the pupil is willing to read aloud. Some would prefer to do so and not be treated differently from the rest of the class. Others are very conscious that their reading skills are laboured and this anxiety can make their reading worse.

♦ When reading textbooks, introduce the content, so students become tuned in to the gist of the material and keywords. This will help with comprehension. If it is a text with questions at the end of sections, get students to read the questions before reading the text, so they know what points are relevant.

♦ Be understanding when giving poetry or other sequences to be learnt off-by-heart. Some students find it exceptionally difficult to remember a sequence regardless of how much time they spend on it. Some do not register rhyme as a pattern. In learning poetry, if a verse has line endings such as: 'hood', 'good', 'wood', they are as likely to say 'forest' for 'wood'. They have understood the poem and know the ideas and content but they may not perceive the rhyming pattern.

♦ If students have difficulty in structuring what they want to say, arrange to give extra time so they can get their thoughts together. The same applies when asking a question. Remember some students have to decipher the question and then formulate their answer. This can put them under time pressure and adds to their anxieties and frustration in the class. Anxiety can mean they cannot retrieve the information when it is needed. They can spend a lot of time worrying about being asked questions. Under pressure they can resort to wild guesses. One technique which would help is if the teacher arranges with them (privately) that they will be asked questions only when the teacher is standing in a particular place. This will mean they can relax for the rest of the time and concentrate on what is being said. Another technique when asking them a question is for the teacher to ask the question, turn and write something on the board and then look for the answer. Students have then had time to put their thoughts together.

♦ Some students have difficulty recalling the name of an object or person. Students could know all about Leonardo Da Vinci and yet have difficulty recalling his name. They might guess wildly or else pepper their description of Leonardo's work and times with 'you know your man'. Such students should overlearn the names of people and objects. One method of doing this is to use vocabulary notebooks which contain new words and names in each subject. These can form the basis for revision just before an exam as it is these words that are most likely to have been forgotten.

♦ This next point is one that applies to me personally. I get totally mixed up about right and left. When being taught anything to do with motor skills, such as gym, using a computer mouse or learning to drive, I have to interpret and decipher what the instructor says. If the gym instructor says 'do this', and does a particular action, I have to break it down, analyse what has been done and work out how I have to move to copy it. Once I have learnt how to do an action, it becomes automatic. This illustrates the point that students who may not have academic difficulties may still be affected in other subjects with a motor skills element such as Physical Education, Home Economics, Technical Graphics, Science or Art. They have to interpret what they are being asked to do and then work out how to do it. It is as though they have to translate the instruction before doing it. This can make them appear slow and lacking in concentration.

♦ When correcting, be sparing in the use of red pen. Not all mistakes need to be marked. Take a particular category of error and correct it. There is a greater possibility that the student will learn from this. A comment such 'improve your writing' will have little effect on the standard of writing. Students may not know how to improve their handwriting. Try to identify one fault which they can work on such as 'closing the loops in letters such as a, d, g'. Remember it will have taken students longer than their classmates to produce this homework and it is disheartening if it is full of corrections. Students will learn more if one or two class of error are marked and then positive instructions are given on how to correct it. If the idea is right, give marks regardless of spelling, layout and presentation. Take time to check out bizarre spellings. Since self-esteem can be low, positive encouragement is needed, which is why it is so important that students gets credit for work done. However for self-esteem to be fostered, the achievement of the pupil must be real. Students will be aware if praise is given for poor work and they could become cynical.

This will mean they may not believe genuine praise given to worthwhile work.

♦ Order and structure may need to be taught to some students whereas most students at second-level have learnt how to lay out their work and organise their studies. Some ideas here would be to use Maths copies with squared paper to help keep figures in columns. Take students aside and show them how you want a page laid out. Write out an example to which students can refer.

♦ Since some students with dyslexia have a poor grip of the pen, which causes muscle strain, pens with padded tops can be helpful.

♦ Give students a structure for attempting longer written answers. Too often answers will be too short because they do not develop a structure. They feel if they think of one point, it is sufficient, instead of attempting to show all they know about a topic. Mindmaps are a very useful technique here. Show them how to sketch out answers and the points they need to include before they start to write their answer.

♦ If spelling is a problem, students should use a vocabulary notebook in each subject. When students come across a new word, they should enter it into the notebook. Encourage the student to learn the spellings in this notebook. Use of multi-sensory teaching of spellings will help retention. This could involve the following steps

1. Students look at the word picking out any difficult parts of the word.

2. They say the spelling.

3. They trace the spelling. If students are asked to write the spelling out ten times, very often they will begin to spell the work incorrectly. Tracing means the word remains correct.

4. Students now write the spelling from memory.

5. They check if it is correct.

6. They then use the word in a sentence.

♦ Encourage the student to use computers. Accept homework done in this format, as long as it is filed in an organised way. Computers can liberate the student with dyslexia. The only drawback to this is the fact that the student might not have the use of a computer in the state examinations as the numbers granted such an accommodation are quite low.

♦ Because students with dyslexia can tend to be disorganised and lack structure in their work, they need very clear guidelines and revision plans. Before an exam, write out the main headings of the material that will be examined, so they have a precise agenda. The clearer this is, the better. Allocate sections of work to particular weeks. Within a chapter, give the major headings for revision. These students benefit enormously from study skills workshops.

♦ Multi-sensory teaching can help learning. If lessons include written, oral and visual elements, these provide more 'hooks' for the student to remember the content.

♦ Write clearly on the board. Give plenty of time to take down the information. Students with dyslexia may find this task difficult. Owing to poor memory skills, they may take down a smaller section of material than others each time. They have to look at the board more frequently. They also may have difficulty finding their place when looking back at the board. They may also have difficulty deciphering script handwriting.

♦ Make sure students have a 'picture' of the course being covered. When introducing new work, give an overview of the topic. It can help students see the structure and can draw the different strands together for them.

♦ Listen to what parents say about the student. Take into consideration their views on which teaching methods are successful. They have had the closest contact with the student and also may have to participate more often in homework than the parents of students without learning difficulties.

♦ Changing the format of the class to include co-operative learning strategies such as peer tutoring, active learning and discovery learning can positive interactions in the classroom.

In co-operative learning students share knowledge with other students though a variety of structures. *The Post-Primary Guidelines on Inclusion* include a comprehensive section on such strategies.

♦ Look for suggestions in the psycho-educational assessment on what teaching strategies may work with the particular student.

♦ Besides listening to the student, parents and the psychologist about the most appropriate and successful approaches to learning and exams, the teacher also needs to develop his/her own ideas on what will work with the student.

It cannot be denied that meeting the needs of a student with dyslexia in the classroom will place enormous demands on the teacher who will need empathy, patience, extra time and imagination to present the courses in different ways. Many teachers are already stressed with the demands made upon them.

In justice, such students deserve that the school system is supportive of their needs and that their teachers, if they find the students cannot learn the way they normally teach, look for different methodologies to teach them the way they can learn. The thrust of the Education Act 1998 and the Task Force Report stresses the rights of the students for appropriate education. Subject teachers, who must meet the demands of the state exam system, realistically may find it difficult to give enough individual attention to one particular student who experiences learning difficulties. On the other hand, a teacher, who has an understanding of the dyslexia and adapts teaching strategies as much as possible, will do much for such students.

There is also a reward for the teacher when these students do achieve. Students with dyslexia can be enthusiastic learners when they find techniques that work for them. Since they are often of average or above-average intelligence and have only been held back by their verbal difficulties, they can make very good progress, which is hugely satisfying for the students, their parents and their teachers. With increasing confidence and new learning strategies, students with dyslexia can confound earlier predictions about their achievement.

Options After Junior Certificate

10

The ESRI survey published in 2004 on the Economic Status of School-leavers highlights the fact that one in five young people continues to leave formal education before completion of the Leaving Certificate. The majority of these are absorbed into the workforce, generally into low pay, low skill and frequently temporary employment. It states that many young people who are entering the labour market do not have the skills or resources to maintain any long-term position in it. For those early school leavers who do obtain employment there are significant pay differentials in rates of pay between those who leave school with a Leaving Certificate and those who do not.

I would never advise students to leave school after their Junior Certificate unless they have plans that will further their qualifications and skills. It need not necessarily be a traditional Leaving Certificate. Options available include:

♦ Apprenticeships.
♦ Youthreach.
♦ Employment.
♦ Failte Ireland.
♦ National Learning Network.
♦ Leaving Certificate Traditional.
♦ Leaving Certificate Applied.
♦ Leaving Certificate Vocational.

APPRENTICESHIPS

Apprenticeship is the route to becoming a skilled craftsperson. The apprentice works for an employer in a chosen occupation and learns the necessary skills and knowledge. Apprenticeships are standard-based. This means apprentices will have specific tests and assessments to ensure they meet certain pre-set standards of competency and skill. Apprenticeships comprise on-the-job training with the employer and off-the-job training in a FAS training centre or in an educational college.

The entry requirements for apprenticeships are that the applicant has reached 16 years of age and has obtained a D grade in five subjects at Junior Certificate level. Although Junior Certificate is the minimum requirement for entry, in 2007 over 60% of new apprentices actually have a Leaving Certificate qualification. As apprentices must pass the tests and assessments, the improved literacy and numeracy skills due to having completed a Leaving Certificate will be of great benefit to them on the apprenticeship course. Students with the minimum qualifications of five D's in the Junior Certificate will struggle with the demands of the apprenticeship course.

There are three routes to an apprenticeship place:

♦ Some apprenticeships, such as the ESB, the Army and Aircorps, will be advertised in the national papers. If the apprenticeship is advertised in the national papers, the number of applicants rises. Apprenticeship places in state employment are advertised.

♦ Register with the local FAS office. It might have details of employers looking for apprenticeships.

♦ Apply directly to local firms. The FAS office and the Golden Pages may help when compiling a list of firms.

If a student is offered an apprenticeship, it is important to check that it is a fully recognised apprenticeship, that the student will achieve certification at the end of the period and the firm will allow time for off-the-job training. Also check that the student would be kept on for the full training period. Within two weeks of starting an apprenticeship, the apprentice should register with FAS. FAS encourages girls to apply for apprenticeship places including offering a bursary to employers.

RACE, Curragh House, Kildare, offers apprenticeship training for jockeys.

YOUTHREACH

Young people who leave school without any qualification or with a Junior Certificate only are the most vulnerable in the job market. Statistics show the highest unemployment and lowest wages are amongst this group. Youthreach is a special programme sponsored by the Department of Education and Science and the Department of Enterprise, Trade and Employment to give early school-leavers a second chance.

Youthreach (www.youthreach.ie) offers young people an opportunity to gain qualifications and build self-confidence so they can move on into further education, training or work. It offers a range of qualifications including FETAC, City and Guilds, and Junior and Leaving Certificates. Youthreach is available in ninety FAS and VEC funded centres. The training and work experience lasts two years for those with no educational qualification and nineteen months for those with a Junior Certificate. Trainees receive regular FAS allowances depending on age.

EMPLOYMENT

While there is more employment available in recent years for students with no qualifications or with only their Junior Certificate, the work is mostly low wage employment, much of it part-time or temporary, with poor prospects of training or promotion.

FÁILTE IRELAND

The hotel, catering and tourism industry needs trained staff to work in bars, restaurants, guesthouses and hotels throughout Ireland. Fáilte Ireland is responsible for training people, giving them the skills, information and opportunities they need in order to fill these jobs.

Fáilte Ireland (www.failteireland.ie/training skills) runs training courses nationwide. Courses include skills training, professional cookery, tourism, hospitality and bar and restaurant management. Participants receive free training and a training and travel allowance. An EU recognised qualification is gained. Applicants should be seventeen years old (eighteen in the case of bar courses).

Courses are also offered in the institutes of technology through the CAO system.

NATIONAL LEARNING NETWORK

National Learning Network (formerly called NTDI) is Ireland's largest non-Government training organisation with more than fifty purpose-built training and employment facilities catering for around 4,500 students each year. The organisation offers over forty different vocational programmes which carry nationally and internationally recognised certification and are designed to lead directly to jobs or progression to further education.

There are no formal entry qualifications to any NLN courses. Applicants must be over sixteen, be eligible for European Social Fund funding and be approved by the National Disability Authority. Applications from dyslexic students are considered for these courses.

All National Learning Network (**www.nln.ie)** courses are designed to prepare students for the world of work and involve assessment, theory and practical training. Qualifications which have credibility with employers and which accurately reflect the scope and level of each individual's abilities and achievements is vital for all those trying to access the jobs market. Certifying bodies include FETAC, FAS, City & Guilds, Failte Ireland, National Tourism Certificate Board, Teagasc, European Computer Driving Licence, Pitman's Examining Institute, University of Cambridge, Institute of Accounting Technicians of Ireland, Royal Horticultural Society and the National Retail Training Council.

For the student with severe dyslexia who is having enormous difficulty coping with the demands of second-level school, these courses provide a route to qualifications and skills.

LEAVING CERTIFICATE EXAMINATION

Since 1995 there are three types of Leaving Certificate provided for students in senior cycle.

◆ The established Leaving Certificate. Students do a two-year course of study and there is a final examination at the end of the two years. Most students take seven subjects. Subjects are offered at two levels, higher and ordinary. In Irish and Maths, foundation level is also offered. It would be expected that a student who did foundation level in these two subjects for Junior Certificate would take this level, as well as students who might find the subjects exceptionally difficult at senior level. *Foundation level Maths and Irish are not acceptable for entry to the majority of CAO courses.* The entry requirement for the vast majority of higher certificate courses in the institutes of technology is that the student should have five subjects in the Leaving Certificate including a D in *English or Irish* and in Maths. A decision that students should take foundation level Maths might be made in second year. Students and parents often may not realise that the consequence of this decision which is that the student is not eligible for courses in the institutes of technology after Leaving Certificate.

♦ Leaving Certificate Applied (LCA). This is a two year self-contained programme. Its objective is to prepare participants for adult and working life. It has three main elements:

♦ Vocational preparation which focuses on the preparation for work, work experience, enterprise and communications.

  ✧ Vocational education which gives students general life skills, including the arts, social education, leisure and languages.

  ✧ General education which is concerned with the development of mathematical, information technology and practical skills necessary for specialist areas such as tourism, business, horticulture, engineering and technology.

Students are assessed throughout the two years, they receive credit for completing modules of the course and there are exams at the end of the two years. After finishing the course, the students may go on to employment or to Post Leaving Certificate (PLC) courses. Since they have not sat a traditional Leaving Certificate examination, they are not eligible to apply for CAO courses directly as the points system does not apply to the LCA. However a student could do a LCA, go on to a PLC and then, on the basis of the PLC result, apply to the institutes of technology through the CAO system. The LCA was offered for the first time in 1996 in about sixty schools. By 2006 approximately 300 hundred schools were offering it. The website www.lca.ie has information about the programme and schools offering it.

♦ Leaving Certificate Vocational (LCV). The objective of this programme is to strengthen the vocational dimension of the Leaving Certificate through relating and integrating specific pairings of subjects. There are link modules to increase the vocational focus of the Leaving Certificate. The student takes a minimum of five subjects and these include Irish and a foreign language. Subjects which complement one another are grouped together and the student takes a particular group of subjects such as Engineering and Technical Drawing or Home Economics and Biology. There are link modules covering preparation for work, work experience and enterprise education. Students can apply to the CAO. LCV was available in over 150 schools in 1996 and by 2005 the number had risen to over 500. The Department of Education and Science has the list of schools offering it. If the student is interested in applying for CAO, check if the LCV course has five or six Leaving Certificate subjects. Six subjects are counted for points so taking five subjects may put the student at a disadvantage. When applying to the institutes of technology, a pass grade in the link module is worth 30 points, a merit grade 50 points and a distinction grade 70 points.

SUBJECT CHOICE FOR SENIOR CYCLE

This is a key moment in career choice for students. In Ireland, because students may take seven subjects or more for the Leaving Certificate, it is still possible to leave many paths open and not narrow one's options after the Junior Certificate. This is generally a good thing as it gives students time to mature before making critical career decisions. In the U.K. this is the time when students specialise and take a narrow range of subjects for A levels.

However, in Ireland where such a wide range of subjects is offered, option structures may be restricted and students with dyslexia may be at a disadvantage. They may have to take subjects that are verbally based and may not be able to specialise in their best subjects. As an example of this, take a student with dyslexia who is very proficient in the Maths, Business and Technical subjects. This student may have to take English, Irish and a third language as three of seven subjects.

Unless the option structure is very open, it is possible that other verbally based subjects such as Economics or History may have to be taken. If the same student could choose subjects such as English, Maths, Physics, Chemistry, Accounting, Technical Graphics and Engineering, it would certainly improve the chances of maximising points for the CAO system as well as giving the student subjects which might be more enjoyable to study. The exemptions from Irish and the NUI third language requirement can be of great benefit in allowing the students to concentrate on their best subjects. In Chapter 5 the example is given of a student who, by having an exemption from the third language requirement of NUI and taking two extra subjects outside of school, increased his points by 110 points.

I have always enjoyed working with students as they face the challenge of choosing senior cycle options. It is a time when one sees the adult emerging in students as they face up to making major decisions. Some students can be very mature and have very clear ideas, so subject choice is relatively simple. Others, while they have begun to think about careers, are not ready to narrow their options. It is important that these students do not limit their choice of careers. The Leaving Certificate provides a structure for students to maintain a wide choice. If students take Irish (unless exempt), English and Maths and choose a language, a science and a business subject among their options, most careers and courses are open to them.

Career inventories and questionnaires can help students decide what direction they may take. Such instruments are available on websites such as www.qualifax.ie and www.careerdirections.ie

At this stage, when the student is making choices, parents and students need information on careers and course requirements. This is the time to start a careers file and begin research on colleges and courses. It is necessary to know the requirements for courses.

There are two sets of requirements:

♦ Colleges set minimum entry requirements. An example of this is the institutes of technology which set a requirement of five subjects in the Leaving Certificate with a pass grade in Maths and English or Irish for many of their courses. The Colleges of NUI (UCC, UCD, UCG and Maynooth) specify six subjects, two at higher level, with a pass in English, Irish and a third language. Trinity College Dublin and Limerick University require the student to have English and another language as an entry requirement.

♦ Certain courses have specific entry requirements. These are often related to what the student will be studying, e.g. a course in languages will specify that a student needs a certain grade in that language at Leaving Certificate.

Some examples of subject requirements include:

Maths Higher level Maths is essential for engineering degrees and actuarial studies.
Ordinary level Maths is a minimum requirement for most courses in the institutes of technology courses.

English Higher level English is essential for Clinical Speech in TCD, Journalism in DCU and Communications in DCU.
Ordinary level English is required for a wide range of institute of technology courses.

Irish Higher level Irish is essential for primary teacher training.
Ordinary level Irish is required for entry in NUI colleges unless the student has an exemption from the Department of Education and Science.

Science Science courses will require a science subject. TCD requires two sciences for some medical/paramedical courses. DIT requires higher level Chemistry for Dietetics.

Complete information on course requirements is available in the college brochures. These are available from the admissions office in each college. This information will also be on the websites of the colleges. Go to the CAO website (www.cao.ie) and there are links to the higher educational institutions websites.

The criteria for choosing subjects for Leaving Certificate should include:

- Students should have the essential subjects needed for any courses they may consider doing after Leaving Certificate.
- They choose subjects which will be of interest to them and that they will enjoy. This will help with motivation. Logically these subjects would tally with the strengths shown in profiles of abilities.
- If they are interested in applying for courses in the CAO system, they choose subjects that will give them the best exam grades to maximise points.

Developing a Learning Style

11

Most of the content of this book concentrates on how parents, teachers, school administration and support services can help the student with dyslexia. However students need, as they grow older, to develop ways to help them become independent learners. It is a key step if they are to achieve their potential. This chapter looks at ways to achieve this. It is based on an article that I wrote after the 1999 AGM of the Dyslexia Association. Students with dyslexia were invited to attend and were given a forum for the exchange of views. From the resulting discussion it appeared many of them did not know exactly how dyslexia affected them and what were the most appropriate learning strategies. Some of this confusion is explained by the fact that dyslexia affects each student differently. The psycho-educational assessment can be used to help students understand how dyslexia affects them personally and what are their own particular strengths and weaknesses. The most appropriate learning strategies will depend on these. Many of the students had not read or discussed the contents of the assessment report. It is up to students to test out the possible strategies and decide what works best for them. Below is a list of suggestions for students to consider. It is addressed mainly at the third-level student but many of the suggestions are equally applicable to the second-level student, particularly in senior cycle.

There is a section targeted specifically for students on the *Understanding Dyslexia* CD produced by the Department of Education and Science which is available in all schools. This includes information and strategies that would be of great benefit to students. Topics addressed include:

◆ Why do I learn differently?

♦ Your learning profile.

♦ Asking for help.

♦ In school.

♦ Doing homework.

♦ Study tips and mindmaps.

♦ Using computers and tape recorders.

Organisation of Time, Work and Workplace

♦ Timetable. Have a structured timetable for study from the first day of a course, so steady progress is made. It is more difficult for the student with dyslexia to cram before an exam. It can lead to confusion and feeling of being overwhelmed.

♦ Regular time of day. Check which part of the day suits best for study. Some students find morning the most beneficial, some the evening. Consider the foods and drinks that might affect concentration such as coffee. Lack of food can also do this.

♦ Decide on a given period of time, not too long. Students with dyslexia often have to concentrate harder than other students. If you work for too long, your work and/or concentration may deteriorate and mistakes multiply. For the same reason, try to avoid study when rushed, under pressure or tired.

♦ Set out realistic study goals and priorities.

♦ Keep only one diary for all appointments, dates, exams, assignments, projects, social life, and work commitments. A personal organiser may be useful.

♦ Study at a desk, in a comfortable chair and comfortable clothes with a quiet environment.

Finding Help

♦ Talk to the academic staff and disability support staff in the institution about the support services and your needs.

♦ Seek assistance from a counsellor, tutor or mentor who could help you develop strategies for learning more effectively. Do this when the course begins and don't wait until you are in trouble and overwhelmed by the demands of the course.

♦ Ask the following be given to you in writing:
   ✧ Booklists, course outlines and schedules of assignment dates.
   ✧ Timetables, late changes in the timetable and exam timetable.
   ✧ Guidelines on how to present out assignments, bibliographies, footnotes, etc.
   ✧ Feedback on completed assignments.
   ✧ Practice exam questions that demonstrate exam format.

♦ Join or form a co-operative learning group.

♦ Ask someone to proofread essays or projects before handing them up. It would be useful if such work was discussed with a tutor prior to preliminary drafting and that the early assignments are checked by a tutor prior to submission. Such supports are available in some colleges.

♦ Sometimes the student may encounter a lecturer who is not aware of the range of difficulties that a student with dyslexia may have. Be prepared and have information on the topic ready to hand out and then be ready to explain how you are affected.

♦ The *Understanding Dyslexia* CD has a very useful form for students when asking teachers for help. Students may be embarrassed and it can be hard to find the necessary words while not appearing to be criticising the teacher. The form provides a neutral mechanism to help this communication.

Asking for Help Form

To_____(teacher's name)

From _____(pupil's name)

---

1. I think I could do better in your class if you
   ✧ Let me work with a 'support buddy'.
   ✧ Let me sit in the front nearer to your desk.
   ✧ Gave me more time to answer questions and do my work.

✧ Gave me more help in the classroom when I don't know what to do.

✧ Showed me how to do things rather than just telling me.

✧ Let me photocopy the overheads or lecture notes.

✧ Gave more information on handouts.

✧ Used more visual information like illustrations, graphs, maps charts, videos, photographs and posters.

✧ Used simpler words when explaining things.

✧ Spoke slower.

✧ Would give instructions one at a time and repeat them.

✧ Let me use a coloured overlay in class when I read.

✧ Told me I didn't have to read out aloud in front of the class.

✧ Gave me more time to read.

✧ Let me tape record the class lesson.

✧ Let me use a computer to help me do my work.

✧ Let me use a dictaphone or tape recorder.

2. I think I could do better if, when you made worksheets, you

✧ Used a bigger and clearer font like Arial, Comic Sans MS or Sassoon Primary in size 12 -16 with double spacing.

✧ Used words that were easier for me to read.

✧ Printed on light coloured paper.

3. I think I could do better if, when you use the board or overhead projector, you

✧ Printed rather than used joined/cursive writing.

✧ Used colour chalk or markers.

✧ Read slowly or repeated whatever you write.

✧ Wrote less for me to copy.

4. I think I could do better with your homework if you

✧ Let me hand in work as mindmaps.

✧ Let me write less than the others.

✧ Let me just write the answers and not the questions.

✧ Let me memorise less.

✧ Let me check with you to see if I wrote down the homework right.

✧ Let me do my homework on my computer.

✦ Let me do my homework on my tape recorder.

5. I think I could do better in your tests if you
    ✦ Read the test questions aloud before the test.
    ✦ Gave me more time to do tests.
    ✦ Let me do the test orally.

Taken from *Understanding Dyslexia* CD (Department of Education and Science) 2005

STUDY METHODS

♦ Become computer literate as soon as possible, preferably early on at second-level. By the time you reach third-level, you should ensure your computer skills are excellent. You may find it easier to study lecture notes that have been entered on a computer, the print being more legible than handwriting. Do you have the skills to use a laptop in lectures? Will lecturers give you permission to do so? If not, enter the notes on the computer the same evening as the lecture, when the notes are still fresh in your mind.

♦ Check if assistive technology can help you. Read the chapter on computers to check out what is available.

♦ Do prescribed reading in advance so you are prepared for lectures. It will make you familiar with main topics and key words and will help with spelling new vocabulary.

♦ Sit in the front of the room where visual and auditory cues are clearer and it is easier to concentrate on the content of the lecture.

♦ Attend every class, tutorial, and laboratory session. Much of your learning will result from the lecture presentation where learning can be facilitated by the visual, aural and written elements. Students with dyslexia usually have more difficulty catching up on missed lectures from other students' notes that are only in written form.

♦ If taking notes by hand, ensure you take down the main points and structure of what a lecturer is saying. Use mindmaps or headings, sub headings and points. Leave plenty of space, so you can expand on points later. If a lecturer uses a word you cannot spell, write it phonically and circle or mark it. This means you will not waste time wondering how to spell it and lose the thread of the lecture. Listen carefully to the opening remarks of the lecturer. Good lecturers will state the purpose of the lecture and will sum up at the end. They may also give clear guidelines that help with notes such as enumerating the number of points to be made. If your handwriting is difficult to read, perhaps ask a fellow-student to take a carbon copy or photocopy his/her notes. Don't miss the lecture if you are doing this.

♦ Ask lecturers prior to the lecture for the notes or a copy of the overhead slides they will be using. It means less writing and you can listen and concentrate on what is said. The structure and sequence of the lecture will be clearly laid out. It is also possible to include additional notes or points where relevant.

♦ Tape lectures (with prior permission). You can concentrate on listening to the lecture to understand it and use the tape to make notes that evening. You will need a good mike to cut out background noise and sit at the front of the room. Label the tape clearly. It may provide a welcome break from reading to listen to such work.

♦ Transcribe or refine notes as soon as possible after a lecture to ensure they are legible and structured and that you understand the points in them.

♦ Write down questions or points not understood for discussion later with the tutor or lecturer.

♦ Develop a shorthand for keywords which help to minimise writing such as envr for environment.

♦ Ask lecturers to shorten booklists so that the essential texts are clearly marked.

♦ Ensure you understand the essay, project, or assessment requirements before you start.

♦ Use a reader service or ask to have essential texts audio-taped.

SPECIFIC STRATEGIES

Students who learn aurally

If you learn more through aural than from written information, think of using tapes of lectures, taping notes and find out if any of your texts are available on tape. Get involved in discussions of topics with lecturers and fellow students. Repeat material to be learnt aloud. Read drafts of essays aloud to see if they make sense.

Students who learn visually

Some students have a strong visual memory. This can be used when learning. Such students are able to recall the look of a page of notes. This assists in the recall of the content of the page. Make use of colour, numbering of points, margins, headings and diagrams when making notes. Mindmaps will be very useful here.

Difficulty with text

Some students may have difficulty in deciphering the meaning of complex texts. They may have to reread pages several times. This may as a result of the number of clauses in each sentence or new vocabulary. Ask for help and direction. Ask that reading lists highlight the essential texts to be read. Always know your purpose in reading a text. Make notes showing the development of the points in the text. Reading the text aloud may help in comprehension. If the type is very small, have it enlarged. Do your reading early in the day, because if you are tired, it can become more difficult to concentrate.

The *Kurzweil* is a computer programme that scans text and reads aloud. This could be particularly useful. *Read and Write Gold* is a programme that reads any material on the computer screen aloud including internet pages.

Spelling

If spelling difficulties remain, develop strategies to cope. Ask others to proofread documents. Use the spell check on the computer or a Franklin word master. Keep a list of new words and learn them off by heart. Inform the academic staff of the difficulties and give examples of your spelling. Ask that your examiners be informed of the difficulties. In a number of courses spelling might be critical to success such as medical or paramedical courses where the correct spelling of drugs or conditions is essential or teaching where the teacher will be expected to be able to spell correctly before a class. In these cases it will be necessary to develop spelling strategies for accuracy. Gilroy & Miles in *Dyslexia at College* have a useful chapter on this topic.

Memory Difficulties

- Some students find it difficult to retain information over time. Strategies that might help include:

- Good note-taking skills so the notes are clear and comprehensible.

- Learning the notes. Some students feel that once the notes are made and filed, that the work is done. Notes must be learnt. This learning can be checked by an oral recital or writing them out again. Mnemonics may help with learning.

- A revision plan where the topic is revised on a frequent basis. Such a plan could entail learning the material on the night of the lecture, a weekly revision of all new material learnt and a monthly revision of the month's work. Each time you revise it will take a shorter time.

- Make sure you understand what you are learning, as this makes it easier to memorise.

Options after leaving certificate

12

Here again it is obvious from statistics that the longer the student remains in education the greater are the opportunities open to him. The ESRI survey published in 2004 on the Economic Status of School-leavers shows that the expanding economy has provided an increase in employment for school-leavers with Leaving Certificate qualifications since 1994. The survey also showed how the results in the Leaving Certificate affect employment opportunities. The better the results, the lower the rate of unemployment and the better the rate of pay.

The choices available after Leaving Certificate have improved for all students including the student with dyslexia. There are more employment, new courses, more places on courses, new routes to qualifications and the provision of more support services in colleges. It is a rapidly changing sector of education.

Although it is often suggested that there is a shortage of places on courses for students after Leaving Certificate, this is not the reality. There are a limited number of places on certain high demand courses such as Medicine, Law, Veterinary and Pharmacy. This scarcity of places raises the points for these courses. However there are plenty of places on courses available for school-leavers after the Leaving Certificate. In 2007 close to 50,000 students sat the Leaving Certificate. There were approximately 32,000 places available in the CAO system. There were another 16,000 places available in the PLC system. So, between the PLC and CAO systems, there were plenty of places in further and higher education for Leaving Certificate cohort. This does not include the other application systems open to students such as Failte Ireland, Teagasc, FAS apprenticeships and the U.K. colleges.

The main routes for a student seeking qualifications after Leaving Certificate are:

- The Central Applications Office (CAO): courses at honours degree, ordinary degree and higher certificate level in universities, institutes of technology, nursing, and some other colleges.
- Post Leaving Certificate courses (PLCs).
- UCAS: the U.K. application system.
- Failte Ireland: hotel, catering and tourism courses.
- Teagasc: agriculture and horticulture courses.
- FAS: apprenticeships and training courses.

These courses fit into the National Framework of Qualifications (www.nfq.ie) which was launched in 2003. It is a system of ten levels that incorporates awards made for all kinds of learning, wherever it is gained. The NFQ, through its ten levels, provides a means of comparing and contrasting national and international education and training qualifications. It helps learners to plan their education and training and employers to identify the qualifications they require.

School, further education and higher education are all included. For Leaving Certificate students the relevant levels are:

- PLC courses   Level 5 and some at level 6
- CAO Higher Certificate   Level 6
- CAO Ordinary Degree   Level 7
- CAO Honours Degree   Level 8.

THE CENTRAL APPLICATIONS OFFICE (CAO)

This is the main application system for Leaving Certificate students. It covers approximately 32,000 places on courses in over forty higher educational institutions. It is a joint application system for degree and higher certificate level courses. The courses offered are in the universities, institutes of technology, teacher training and some of the private colleges. It is important to remember that fees are payable for courses in private colleges although tax relief can be claimed. It is a single application form. The student can apply for up to ten level 8 courses and ten level 6/7 courses, a total of twenty courses.

The CAO handbook sets out the precise application procedures to be followed and is available from October. The important dates to remember are the closing date, 1st February and late closing date 1st May. If students wish to change their order of preference on the list of courses or to introduce new courses, there is a change-of-mind facility up to 1st July. There are a small number of courses that have additional selection procedures, such as aptitude tests or portfolios. These courses must be included prior to 1st February and it is not possible to introduce these courses on a change-of-mind slip. Offers of places are determined by points for the vast majority of courses provided the student satisfies the college entry requirements and any specified course requirements. The points from the previous year can be used as a rough guide when looking at courses but the points are set each year by the number of places on the course and the number of applicants.

Eligible applicants are placed in an order of merit list for each course to which they have applied. For those presenting Irish Leaving Certificate the majority of courses will be determined by a points score based on examination results (see Fig. 12.1). The greater the points score, the higher an applicant appears in the order of merit list for the course. Places are offered to an appropriate number of applicants, beginning with those at the top of the order of merit list and descending. The points score for a course is the lowest number of points at which a place on that course was offered.

Fig. 12.1: The Points System

Leaving Certificate grade	Higher level	Ordinary level	Bonus
A1	100	60	0
A2	90	50	35
B1	85	45	30
B2	80	40	25
B3	75	35	20
C1	70	30	15
C2	65	25	10
C3	60	20	5
D1	55	15	
D2	50	10	
D3	45	5	

The best six results in recognised subjects are counted for points calculation. Bonus points for Higher Maths are awarded by the University of Limerick. Only one sitting of the Leaving Certificate will count for points.

The CAO handbook gives full details of the application system and is very detailed. It should be consulted by anyone applying to the system. There are some points particularly relevant to students with dyslexia.

♦ It is very important that decisions about colleges and courses are thoroughly researched. The student should collect relevant college brochures, attend open days, and talk to the staff at the colleges and to students attending the courses. It means reading the brochures and knowing the content of the courses in which the student is interested. The same course title can differ in content from college to college. An example of this is a Higher Certificate in Business Studies. In some colleges it includes the study of a language and in others it does not.

♦ The structure of the course can be important for the student with dyslexia. Continuous assessment is a system where assignments are graded throughout the year and form part of the final assessment. Semesters mean that the year's work may be broken into two halves and examined separately. Both continuous assessment and semesters can help the student with dyslexia, by spreading the academic burden throughout the year and reducing the amount to be memorised for an exam. Some courses in certain disciplines are taught through lectures and practicals, where the student can apply the knowledge gained. This hands-on experience provides multi-sensory teaching that can help the student with dyslexia. Other courses may be taught through lectures and reading lists. This may pose greater difficulty for the student, who may need help in reducing the reading list to the essential texts.

♦ The opportunities available in the CAO system are not only for students who get several honours in the Leaving Certificate. In 2007 there were approximately one hundred and forty courses at level six and seven in the CAO system that were offered at 200 points or below. This equates to a Leaving Certificate with one or two honours or high grades in pass subjects. Over forty courses were offered to all qualified applicants. This means students with 5 Ds on ordinary level papers including English and Maths would qualify for a place.

While this is rare, it is possible and the system is flexible enough for students to go as far as their abilities allow. This opens opportunities to the student with dyslexia. Students may not obtain the points to obtain a level 8 course from the Leaving Certificate results, perhaps due to the number of verbally based subjects they have to take. They may obtain a place on a level 6 certificate level course which allows progression to level 7 and level 8.

♦ Use the CAO system fully. This means applying for the twenty courses between both lists. Do not restrict the choice to one location. It is a very noticeable trend that Dublin students do not apply on a national basis but tend to apply to Dublin colleges only. They place themselves at a disadvantage in so doing. The points for courses in Dublin are usually higher than for the same course outside the Dublin area. Take the case of a student interested in Engineering. At level 8 in 2007 the points ranged from 520 for Civil and Environmental Engineering in UCC to 260 for Mechanical and Manufacturing Engineering in Waterford. At level 6/7, the points ranged from 400 for Civil Engineering in DIT to courses where all qualified applicants (those with five passes including English and Maths) got places.

♦ On both the level 8 list and the level 6/7 list students should put the courses in order of preference. <u>It is important that choices be in order of preference the entire way down each list</u>. It is sensible to use the ninth and tenth preference on each list for courses they may consider taking if Leaving Certificate results are lower than expected. For example, a student may wish to do an engineering course in Dublin and will list these courses among the top preferences and then add courses with lower points as a lower preference as an insurance.

♦ Points do not give a ranking to how good a course is. They are a reflection of the number of students applying for that particular course in a particular year. Remember points will vary from year to year but there are patterns to be seen. One pattern is that students prefer to take a course in large cities that have a thriving student population. In the case of the

Higher Certificate in Computing, the same qualification is offered in many of the institutes of technology. The student may need more points to get a place in Dublin, Cork or Galway and yet the student who studies in other colleges obtains the same qualification.

♦ Even if students feel confident about obtaining CAO places, they could also apply to PLC courses as a precaution. Places on such courses may be turned down in September by the student if they have an alternative course but it may not be possible to apply for them at this stage. It is possible to apply to CAO the following year using PLC results.

♦ The CAO and NFQ structure are very flexible. Students can do a two-year level 6 course. If they obtain the necessary results they can do one more year and get an ordinary degree (level 7). After which it may be possible to proceed to an honours degree (level 8). The CAO handbook indicates courses where such progression is possible.

♦ It might also be possible to transfer to university after completing level 6 or level 7 in an institute of technology. The transfer is based on the student's results but it applies to certain faculties only, such as Business Studies, Computing, Science and Engineering.

♦ ACCS is a system which allows part-time students acquire nationally recognised qualifications in the institutes of technology. This can provide another route to qualifications.

SUPPORT SERVICES FOR STUDENTS AT THIRD-LEVEL
AHEAD

In recent years colleges at third-level have become more aware of dyslexia and the difficulties faced by students with dyslexia. In my opinion there has been much more development in support services at this level than at second-level. This development of services has been supported by the work of AHEAD (Association for Higher Education Access and Disability). AHEAD works to promote full access to and participation in third-level education for students with disabilities in Ireland. Their website www.ahead.ie includes

♦ Up-to-date information on all issues relating to disability and third-level education.

♦ Information on publications issued both through AHEAD and other organisations.

♦ A disability information section provides information on the various different types of disabilities as well as information on third-level college resources for students with disabilities. This section is aimed at both students and teachers.

♦ A student support section which contains information on supports available for students and graduates such as mentoring programmes and a 'Got a query?' service.

It also provides a link to the Inclusive Education Information Centre, which provides factsheets on accessing third-level education, including sample SIF forms showing the type of information which the school and student should include on the form.

The Supplementary Information Form

The Supplementary Admission Route facilitates access to higher education institutions for applicants, who may not meet the CAO points for the course of their choice on account of a disability. In some cases the points level for a particular course may be reduced for a student. While in the past each college has its own procedures for assessing students, in 2006 eight colleges became involved in a common approach. It is very likely that more will join this initiative. The colleges were

♦ Athlone Institute of Technology

♦ Dublin City University

♦ Dublin Institute of Technology

♦ National University of Ireland, Maynooth

♦ Trinity College, Dublin

♦ University College Cork

♦ University College, Dublin

♦ University of Limerick

Whether it is an individual college or this joint initiative, the steps in the procedure are very similar.

Each student must reach at least the minimum entry requirements for their course and any specific course requirements. Students who have a language exemption must apply directly to the participating colleges to have it recognised. This means a student with an Irish exemption from the Department of Education must apply to NUI to have the exemption recognised.

The steps in making the supplementary admission application are:

1. Complete the standard CAO form.

2. The student discloses his/her specific learning disability on the CAO by ticking the box on the form.

3. The student will receive a separate Supplementary Information Form (SIF).

4. The student must complete and return the form by the required date in March.

The information required for the form includes:

♦ Details of the disability.

♦ Details of the supports the student received at school.

♦ Likely supports needed in higher education.

♦ School academic reference.

♦ In the case of dyslexia, a recent psycho-educational assessment. Reports that are older than three years old will not be accepted, and the application will not be considered.

The forms are forwarded by the CAO to the participating colleges who review all the applicants. It means that individual applicants are considered in relation to the impact their disability had on their education. The only evidence in front of the group in making a judgement about the student is the SIF and the accompanying documentation so it is critically important that the student and the school complete the SIF thoroughly and give all relevant information. Based on the SIF the group will prioritise students into three levels in relation to the impact of their disability on second-level education. Priority for intervention on the points levels for courses will be given to students at level two and level three.

It is really important that time and effort goes into completing the SIF, ensuring all relevant information is included from both the personal statement of the student and on the section filled in from the school. The Inclusive Education Information Centre (accessed through the AHEAD website: www.ahead.ie) discusses how to fill in the SIF and has examples of the student and school forms.

The format of the psycho-educational assessment report

Each year some applications are rejected because reports are too old (not within the previous three years) or they are not in the correct format. Information may be inadequate or not relevant. The assessment must be done by a fully qualified psychologist with a recognised qualification. It must be a full assessment. An update or review report is not sufficient.

Preferred tests and format for the psycho-educational assessment are:

- Wechsler Adult Intelligence Scale – Third or Fourth Edition (WAIS III or IV).
- Wechsler Intelligence Scale for Children – Third or Fourth Edition (WISC-III or IV).
- Woodcock Reading Mastery Test Revised – (WRMT-R).
- Wide Range Achievement Test 3 – (WRAT 4).
- Dyslexia Adult Screening Test – (DAST).
- The Adult Reading Test.

Core components of an assessment report should be:

- Cover sheet including the student's name, date of birth, age at assessment, date of assessment, school/college attended.
- Introduction: referral information; family, developmental and educational history; any relevant medical information and the student's perceptions of his/her difficulties. Any previous assessments should be summarised. Where English is spoken as a second or additional language, details of the student's language history and current levels of competence should be included.
- Test behaviour: behaviour during the assessment that may have affected the results.
- General level of intellectual ability: Measures of verbal and non-verbal ability should be reported. The student's profiles of

scores should be discussed, with particular reference to any significant discrepancies between verbal and non verbal ability.

♦ Cognitive processing, including working memory, phonological processing and speed of processing. In some cases a full IQ test (WAIS III UK) will have been administered and reported in the previous section, so some of these aspects may have been covered. Performance in other tests, such as numeracy, motor control and/or attentional functioning, may be included.

♦ Attainments in literacy, including single word reading, non-word reading, text reading and reading comprehension. Results should cover qualitative analysis of errors, evidence of strategies being used, fluency, reading speed and ability to extract information from text. Information about spelling will come from a graded spelling test and from a piece of free writing, which will also yield information about ability to write grammatically, the complexity of sentence structures, the coherence of writing, use of vocabulary, writing speed and legibility of handwriting.

♦ Attainments in Arithmetic should be included if the student will have any mathematical content in their course of study.

♦ Attainments in language and if the student will have difficulty studying a foreign language.

♦ Conclusion: It should be stated whether or not the student has a specific learning difficulty and whether their condition is disabling in the context of studying at third level. The effects of the specific learning difficulty on the student's literacy and study skills should be outlined, taking into account any compensatory strengths.

♦ Recommended support: As students are likely to have an assessment of need at the commencement of their college career, it is not necessary or appropriate to make detailed recommendations about technical support. A brief statement about the type of support which might help the student should be made here, particularly in relation to study skills tuition.

♦ Summary.

It is important that the psychologist knows what the preferred tests and format are, so parents should pass on this information prior to the assessment.

Support while at college

The higher education institutions have disability support officers or access officers who give help, advice and support to students with disabilities. The institutions are anxious to make appropriate provision for such students in good time. The provision of such information does not adversely affect the application in any way. The support services provided by colleges may include:

♦ A waiver of minimum educational requirements for entry for certain courses. The NUI exemption from the 3rd language requirement is an example.

♦ The Supplementary Admission Route as detailed above.

♦ Access to photocopying.

♦ Access to psychological assessment if it is thought the student has undiagnosed dyslexia.

♦ Copies of lecturer's notes.

♦ Study skills tutorials.

♦ Assistance with reading lists to identify key texts.

♦ One-to-one tutorial system.

♦ In-service or information circulated to staff on dyslexia.

♦ Extra time in exams.

♦ Support services in exams such as scribes, readers, taping and use of computers.

♦ Lecturers informed of student's difficulties.

♦ Examiners informed of student's difficulties.

♦ Use of assistive technology such as word processors, voice recognition software, scanners to read text, programmes such as TextHELP.

Students should discuss with the psychologist, parents and/or second level teachers the supports that facilitate their learning styles, so that they are in the position to be able to articulate their needs when asked. They should have considered the supports that are useful for them, both when studying and when taking exams. The Disability Support Services are there to facilitate the student but they do need clear information coming from the assessment and the student about the necessary supports. This reflects the fact that each student with dyslexia has a unique profile of strengths and weaknesses.

POST LEAVING CERTIFICATE COURSES

This is a rapidly developing sector of education. Each year more courses are added to the list and existing courses are further developed. These developments include links to other educational institutions both here and in Britain. While the vast majority of these courses are aimed at the ordinary level Leaving Certificate student who is unlikely to get a CAO place, some have such a high reputation that they could be a student's first option regardless of the CAO place offered. Most PLC courses are level 5 but a small number progress to level 6.

They are primarily designed to prepare students for the world of work and to develop vocational skills. They provide access to employment, further study and further training. PLC courses are available in a wide variety of colleges throughout the country.

Students apply individually to each college. There is no centralised system. Many of the colleges have open days usually in February and March each year. Applications will be accepted from January onwards or at the open days. Closing dates for applications also can vary. Some, particularly for courses with a high demand for places, can be as early as March and in the case of the beautician course in Dun Laoghaire Senior College the closing date is in November. However there can be places available on some courses as late as September.

The selection procedures differ and may include interviews, aptitude tests or the presentation of a portfolio. Some courses are in very high demand, particularly where the college is running a unique course such as the Communications course in Colaiste Dhulaigh or the Animation course in Ballyfermot Senior College. The most common selection procedure is an interview. A portfolio will be needed when applying for Art and Design courses. For

Communication, Radio and TV courses, relevant experience which may form part of a portfolio is desirable. For Journalism, a portfolio of published material is useful.

Since it can be an interview system, this may suit the student with dyslexia who may not have very good grades in the Leaving Certificate but who is articulate and who has gained relevant experience. Work experience, achievements in sport, contribution to the community and award schemes such as An Gaisce (the President's Award Scheme), all can help at interview.

There is a vast range of courses in this sector. Some are available in many PLC colleges, some are unique to one college. They can be classified into main groups as follows:

Art, Craft, Design	Art, Craft, Design, Fashion Design, Interior Design, Computer Aided Design, Furniture Restoration, Animation.
Business	Business, Secretarial, Computer Applications, Marketing, Languages, Retail Studies, Auctioneering, Security.
Science, Technology Natural Resources	Laboratory Techniques, Horticulture, Motor Technology, Food Science, Construction, Electronics Technology, Equestrian Studies.
Services, Leisure Tourism	Hotel, Catering, Tourism, Beauty, Child Care, Nursing Studies, Hairdressing, Tennis Coaching, Marine Skills, Leisure Management, Football, Heritage Studies.
Communications, Drama	Advertising, Journalism, Communications, Video Production, Performing Arts, Languages.

There are increasing links between PLC courses and the colleges in the CAO system. Certification for PLC courses is provided by Further Education and Training Awards Council (FETAC). The website is www.fetac.ie. Since 2005 there are two schemes linking these awards with entry to CAO.

Firstly the Higher Education Links Scheme links PLC courses to places in the universities mainly. There is a quota of places set aside for applicants. Allocation of places is decided on the basis of a grade point average on the eight modules of the PLC course. The PLC course must include modules which are linked to the course being applied for.

Secondly a Pilot Scheme was introduced in 2005 for applicants to level 6 courses in the institutes of technology and some other higher education institutions. Applicants may present results from any PLC course. Points are awarded for the eight modules of the PLC course: 50 points for a distinction, 35 points for a merit grade and 20 points for a pass grade. This means that a student with eight distinction grades obtains 400 points and competes with Leaving Certificate students applying to the CAO on the basis of these points.

Besides the FETAC certification, some PLC courses have recognition from professional bodies such as the Professional Accountancy Bodies or they receive certification from organisations such as City and Guilds. Some courses award British Higher National Diplomas. Some courses allow the student, after successfully completing the PLC, to transfer to a British University.

Usually there are no course fees, although examination and administration fees may have to be paid. Maintenance grants are paid to students. These grants are means tested.

COLLEGES IN THE UK SYSTEM

There is a centralised application system in the UK for both degree and diploma places at university. It is called UCAS (University and College Admissions Service). The website is: www.ucas.com.

The closing date for applications is 15th January, except in the case of Oxford and Cambridge universities and some medical/paramedical courses where the closing date is 15th October. Students apply on-line and list up to five courses. These courses are not in order of preference. The system differs from the CAO in that personal information is included on the application. Students may state their reasons for choosing courses, their relevant work experience, relevant school subjects and their achievements. An academic referee, usually a designated teacher in school, writes a confidential reference on students covering points such as ability, achievement, potential, contribution to school life, any disability and a forecast of Leaving Certificate results.

UCAS sends this information to each college to which the student applied. Each college considers the application and may make a conditional offer. The conditional offer will specify the academic goals to be achieved in the Leaving Certificate. The students know in March or April what results they will need to achieve in the Leaving Certificate to ensure their places on courses. The academic goals set out in each offer may differ depending on the demand for places on the particular course in that college. While students may receive five offers, they can accept two only. Students may choose a college which has set high academic goals in the Leaving Certificate as a firm acceptance and hold a lower offer as insurance in case they do not get the results they hope for in the Leaving Certificate

Applicants who live in the EU must pay towards the tuition fees for each year of the course. Students, who are eligible for Irish Higher Education maintenance grants, can avail of these grants while they attend most courses in the U.K. There are some exceptions to this, so be careful to check that the courses chosen are eligible. Irish Higher Education grants are means-tested.

There are over 80,000 courses in the UCAS system including subjects and subject combinations not available here. There is no change-of-mind facility as there is in the CAO system. This means there is a greater need for detailed research before filling in the application. Students need to know as much as possible about the courses and colleges to which they are applying at this stage. Since applications are submitted in October/January prior to the Leaving Certificate, this research should be started during fifth year.

Reasons why students with dyslexia may consider applying to the U.K.:

♦ Although for high demand courses such as Law, Medicine, Veterinary and Pharmacy entry standards are as high in the U.K. as they are in Ireland, the entrance standards on more general courses such as Computers, Business Studies,

Languages and Engineering may be lower than the equivalent course on the CAO system. One reason for this is the different population structure. In Ireland there is more demand for college places because of the very high proportion of young people in our population.

♦ The support services for students with dyslexia were developed earlier in the UK. However there has been huge progress in Ireland in the provision of supports for students at third-level.

♦ There is a wider range of courses and options within courses available in the U.K.

♦ The Irish application procedure does not allow for information about the student to be included unless one applies as a non-standard applicant by ticking the Medical/Physical/Specific Learning Difficulty box on the CAO form. The U.K. procedure allows for other information both in the student's personal statement and the academic reference. The decision to make an offer takes this information into account. This could be of benefit to a student with dyslexia.

♦ Many Irish applicants use the U.K. system as a form of insurance in case they do not get the place they want in Ireland.

Other sources of information on the U.K. system include:

♦ Philomena Ott's book *How to detect and manage Dyslexia* contains a detailed chapter on further and higher education in the U.K.

♦ SKILL is an organisation in the U.K. similar to AHEAD in Ireland which is concerned about the needs of students with disabilities. It has many publications which could be helpful. Its website is www.skill.org.uk.

♦ In September each year the Institute of Guidance Counsellors, in conjunction with the Irish Times, organise the Higher Options Conference in the R.D.S., Dublin. Many British colleges as well as Irish colleges are represented. It is advisable that students attend this conference. It is held on three separate days. An information night for parents is held during the conference.

AGRICULTURE

Teagasc (www.teagasc.ie) offers a range of agricultural and horticultural courses throughout the country. There are now eleven third-level programmes appearing on the CAO list and this is set to expand in the years ahead.

Teagasc also provides courses that are suitable for people who wish to make a career in agriculture, horticulture, horses or forestry but who do not wish to complete a third-level course and these are nationally accredited by the FETAC. These include:

- Level 4 Certificate in Agriculture.
- Level 5 Certificate in Agriculture.
- Advanced Certificate in Agriculture.
- Advanced Certificate in Agriculture (Part-Time Farmers).
- Advanced Certificate in Dairy Herd Management.
- Advanced Certificate in Drystock Management.
- Advanced Certificate in Agricultural Mechanism.
- Advanced Certificate in Farm Management.
- Advanced Certificate in Machinery and Crop Management.
- Level 4 Certificate in Horticulture.
- Level 5 Certificate in Horticulture.
- Advanced Certificate in Horticulture.
- Advanced Certificate in Horsemanship/Stud Management.
- Level 5/6 Certificate in Forestry.
- Advanced Certificate in Greenkeeping.

There is no minimum educational entry requirement but those who have completed the Leaving Certificate are most likely to benefit. These courses open up a wide range of career options for participants. Many will return to farming either in a full-time or part-time capacity but there are excellent job prospects in the expanding amenity horticulture and forestry sectors.

Paid work experience is an integral part of these courses where participants have the opportunity to develop the skills and competencies associated with their chosen career. Participants who achieve the necessary results may transfer to third level courses and progress up to level 7 or level 8 qualifications.

FAS TRAINING COURSES

Apprenticeship training has been dealt with in Chapter 10. FAS also, through its training centre network, provides close on 170 different training courses of an industrial and commercial nature for unemployed workers, those wishing to update their skills or change their careers and for school-leavers unable to obtain employment.

FAS courses are available to men and women who are unemployed, redundant or out of full-time education. All applicants for FAS courses must register with their local FAS employment services offices.

Training allowances are paid to trainees. Accommodation costs are subsidised for those who must live away from home during the course. For further information, contact the local FAS employment services offices or training centre.

FAS, in conjunction with DAI, run a course called 'Career Path for Dyslexia' (FAS course code AT58F). It is the only course in Ireland catering for the specific needs of unemployed adults with dyslexia. It is run in Celbridge, Co. Kildare. The duration of the course is six months. The course content includes: Health and Safety, Communication, Capacity Building, Personal Development, Information Technology, Literacy Skills, Business Planning, and a work placement.

Choosing a
Career Direction

13

Students are better equipped for the job market if they have further training or education after the Leaving Certificate. This is why the major decision for students in their last year at second-level is the courses they should apply for to continue their education.

There is rapid change and development in the courses provided after the Leaving Certificate. Sometimes when speaking to parents, I am aware that their view of colleges and courses has remained fairly static since the time that they themselves were at school and they still hold the opinions about colleges and qualifications that they held then. This means they can lack an understanding of the complexities of the system and the flexibility of the choices available now. Even as a guidance counsellor it is a major challenge to stay up-to-date with the constant innovation in the provision of courses. To be properly informed, parents need to make themselves aware of the major changes. Some of these changes include:

♦ The major contribution made by the institutes of technology. In some cases employers would look first to these colleges rather than the traditional universities because of the strength of the reputation of certain courses.

♦ The National Framework of Qualifications and the progression routes available for students.

♦ The growth in Post Leaving Certificate courses.

♦ The increasing flexibility and adaptability of the system so students can move from Post Leaving Certificate courses (level 5) to levels 6, 7 and 8. This provides alternative routes to qualifications.

♦ The introduction of systems such as ACCS to aid the part-time student acquire qualifications.

Because of the number of courses and alternative routes to qualifications, students and parents need to research courses. It is not something that should be left to sixth year. It can be difficult to make students realise the urgency to become informed about courses and to begin research. As a guidance counsellor, it is very frustrating to go through the CAO system in detail in the classroom in November and then to have some students wake up in mid-January and come and ask questions about the system when the closing date for applications is 1st February.

The first place to start the research is with the guidance counsellor in the school, who will be able to provide information about colleges, courses, open days and application procedures. The level of provision of a careers service can vary from school to school depending on whether there is a guidance counsellor and the number of hours that are allocated to guidance counselling. Since the guidance counsellor works within the school, he/she will have a good knowledge of the student's abilities, interests and possible results.

The development of the internet has made access to information much easier. The website www.qualifax.ie is the national database of all third level and further education courses. Qualifax is the 'one stop shop' for information on courses for students and has a search facility. Included are links to college and other education / training websites in Ireland and abroad. Detailed information on an extensive selection of careers is supplied, also the definitive calendar of career events, an interest assessment to assist second level students to make career choices, help for students when choosing subjects for senior cycle and a plethora of other useful information for students of all ages.

Further information can be gained from newspapers particularly around mid-August and mid-January. However there can be an element of hyped-up information and headlines can tend to focus on courses where points have risen or the handful of courses that require 500 plus points. Outside the louder headlines, the papers do contain excellent information and sometimes information that is not available elsewhere. This is because of the rapid change in the nature of courses provided and in the job market itself. Publications tend to go out-of-date very quickly. These articles are often accompanied by large advertisements about colleges and courses. Remember that the colleges in highest demand do not need to advertise heavily!

Students should open a careers file and keep all the relevant information in it.

Open days are held from September on. Some schools organise trips to visit colleges. It is possible to get a list of the main open days on the website www.qualifax.ie Major careers events are:

♦ The Higher Options Conference in late-September organised by the Irish Times and the Institute of Guidance Counsellors. Most Irish colleges and many U.K. colleges attend and there is a parents' session one evening. Talks are given on different careers during the day.

♦ In February FAS, in conjunction with the Institute of Guidance Counsellors and the Irish Independent, organise a three-day seminar called Opportunities on careers and employment trends which includes lectures and displays.

If the student or parents are interested in a particular college, ring the college and ask if there is to be an open day. Even if there is not, the staff in the various colleges often make the time available to talk to individual interested students.

Work experience can be another invaluable way to obtain information about careers. I would encourage students to look for work experience during transition year or the summers following transition year or fifth year. It can help them choose a career direction and be of positive benefit if there is an interview for the course.

Of course the key questions are: What courses will students research? What careers interests them? The answer to these questions lie in a process which begins soon after they enter second-level. Some of the constituent factors in making the decision are:

♦ Ability. Each student has different profiles of ability. A test used in many Irish Schools is DATS (Differential Aptitude Testing) which gives a percentile score based on national norms of a student's ability in Verbal Reasoning, Numeric Reasoning, Abstract Reasoning, Spatial Relations, Mechanical Reasoning, Clerical Speed and Accuracy, Spelling and

Grammar. In the case of students with dyslexia, psycho-educational assessments provide much more detailed information on the student's ability and should help the student focus on certain careers and avoid others. These assessments could be even more relevant than the DATS. If the student's profile either from DATS or a psycho-educational assessment has particular strengths and weaknesses, career choices should be centred on the strengths. The student with difficulties in spelling and verbal expression would be wise to avoid careers where verbal skills are important such as office work or journalism. It appears to be a pattern that some students with dyslexia have a strength in spatial relations. This could lead into art, architecture, engineering or design.

♦ Achievement. Achievement is different from ability. Some students with seemingly low levels of ability can achieve very good results because they have the perseverance and motivation to focus on their studies. Other students with excellent ability can do quite badly. A pattern of achievement will be built up by monitoring school reports. Expectations of results in state exams can be based on this. It is highly unlikely that a student who is achieving the grades of 'E' and 'D' during fifth and sixth year will jump to grades of 'A' and 'B' in the Leaving Certificate examination. For most students their grades will be close to their level of achievement in school. This makes it possible to predict the probable range of results in state examinations that a student may achieve. This information can form part of the career decision and helps to make the choice realistic. If a student's results in house exams are around 250 points, the estimated range of the Leaving Certificate results could be between 200 points to 350 points. It is realistic for the student to ensure courses in this range are included on the CAO application. In the CAO system where there are twenty choices, students may still use some of those choices for courses that may go for 400 plus points but they should also ensure they have courses in the range of 200 points.

♦ Interest Testing. These are tests which ask the students questions about careers and indicate their level of interest in different careers groups. These tests are often used at the stage of option choice for senior cycle. In recent years computerised interest tests have become more common. The websites www.qualifax.ie and www.careerdirections.ie have such tests available. Included in some of the interest testing can be questions about the students' interests and personality such as: What do they like to do with their spare time? Do they like to work as part of a team? Do they enjoy organising events? Would they prefer to spend their time mending machines or playing sports or board games? Do they like activities that help care for people such as First Aid or visiting elderly relatives?

♦ Other achievements outside the academic: Have they been involved in sports teams, First Aid, drama, life-saving, sailing or music? How proficient are they in these activities? Do they want this activity to continue as part of their career? Do they have a driving licence? Sometimes leisure interests and achievements provide a route to a career choice.

♦ Work experience will also give students ideas about the type of work they would like to pursue or avoid in the future. It will also provide them with a reference which may be useful at interviews later on.

All these threads; achievement, ability, interests, personality, work experience and other non-academic achievement, form a realistic basis to the process of career decision. It should also provide a list of possible career directions that the student would like to research further. Once students begin to research the courses available and different routes to qualifications, their ideas will be further refined. It is a process that will take time and should be ongoing during all of senior cycle. Preferably it will have started sooner.

Occasionally students will present in sixth year as having no idea as to what career interests them. This can provide a serious obstacle to a discussion. However, if presented with a list of broad career groupings, many of these students have very clear ideas about careers they do **not** want to pursue and it is possible to reduce the list to maybe six broad career headings which they might consider. This provides a good starting point for research.

The above discussion on career choice focuses on the individual's aptitudes, interests and achievements. Another factor to consider is the employment trends. These are notoriously unpredictable. This is because of the changing nature of jobs due to technology and the global market. There are many jobs being advertised now which were not in existence ten years ago. However there are some patterns discernible:

♦ The employment growth which took place during the last ten years in Ireland has provided opportunities for school-leavers. The students who will benefit most will the students with qualifications and/or good skills.

♦ Certain sectors of the economy are providing major employment prospects. In 1998 the Government set up the Expert Group on Future Skills Needs, www.skillsireland.ie. The Group is intended to be the most comprehensive source of all research on labour and skills issues in Ireland. It has identified a number of key occupation/skills areas which are expected to experience skills shortages over the coming years. These include:

✧ Computer and electronics.

✧ Science such as Physicist, Biochemist, etc.

✧ Food science and technology.

✧ Town Planning.

✧ Construction craftspeople.

✧ Manufacturing technology.

✧ Engineering of all types.

✧ Telecommunications.

✧ Financial Services.

✧ Transport.

♦ There is going to be more contract work and fewer permanent appointments. The economy that now exists in Ireland provides the encouraging environment for qualified and skilled workers to set up their own businesses. This is an increasingly attractive option given the growing impermanence of employment.

♦ Because of the developments in technology and resulting changes in job practices, there is a great need for adaptability and flexibility. Workers will need to constantly up-date their skills and information.

Up-to-date information on career trends appears in the newspapers usually in August and January, both critical times for course choices. The FAS Opportunities seminar in February discusses trends in employment. It makes sense that information on employment trends would be part of a decision on career direction.

The Dyslexia Association of Ireland

Appendix

A

The Dyslexia Association of Ireland is a voluntary organisation and a charity. It aims to increase awareness of specific learning disability and promote the welfare of people with dyslexia.

The Association has lobbied for thirty years for the recognition of dyslexia as a major learning difficulty. It has sought the provision of appropriate services by the State for all people with dyslexia. Currently it provides a free public information service and offers psycho-educational assessment to adults and children. It arranges group and individual tuition for children and adults and runs a full-time course for adults in conjunction with FAS. It delivers in-service courses to teachers, speakers to school and parent groups and organises seminars and conferences.

The Association has thirty-four branches, each of which runs group classes for students with dyslexia after school hours. Branches provide local parent support and awareness raising. The Association monitors and evaluates new information and teaching methods for the remediation of specific learning difficulty. It keeps in touch with relevant government departments, professional bodies and educational organisations and represents the views of its members through submissions to government on educational policy.

DAI is a founder member of the European Dyslexia Association and Spectrum, an umbrella group of associations for people with hidden learning difficulties. It has long been a corporate member of the British Dyslexia Association, a member of the Disability Federation of Ireland and the National Adult Literacy Association.

Website: www.dyslexia.ie

National University of Ireland

B

Policy statement on matriculation requirements for students with learning disabilities affecting language acquisition.

The National University of Ireland with its Constituent Universities in Dublin, Cork, Galway and Maynooth is committed to a policy of inclusivity in relation to the admission to the university of students with disabilities and recognises the achievements of the growing numbers of students with disabilities in the university. The NUI has reviewed its matriculation requirements with a view to ensuring that students with certain certifiable learning disabilities, but who, in all other respects, have the capacity to succeed in higher education, are not excluded from matriculation.

The standard matriculation requirements of the National University of Ireland are set out in an annual publication *Minimum Academic Entry and Registration (Matriculation) Requirements.* The NUI recognises that for students with learning difficulties affecting language acquisition, but who in all other respects have the capacity to succeed in higher education, these matriculation requirements may pose particular problems.

The NUI has been influenced by the Association for Higher Education Access and Disability (AHEAD) in accepting the following definition of dyslexia:

Dyslexia is one of several distinct learning disabilities. It is a specific language-based disorder of constitutional origin characterised by disabilities in single word decoding, usually reflecting insufficient phonological processing.

These difficulties in single word decoding are often unexpected in relation to age and other cognitive abilities; they are not the result of generalised developmental disability or sensory impairment.

188

Dyslexia is manifest by variable difficulty with different forms of language, often including, in addition to problems with reading, a conspicuous problem with acquiring proficiency in writing and spelling.

There are special provisions for students whose dyslexia constitutes a significant learning difficulty. A student who has been granted an exemption from Irish at school on the grounds of dyslexia, having been assessed by a professional psychologist, should send a copy of the certificate of exemption, signed by the School Principal, together with the psychologist's report, to NUI. In these cases NUI will grant an exemption from Irish and also from the third language requirement.

Where a student is diagnosed late as having dyslexia and has not come to the attention of the National Educational Psychological Service Agency, NUI will grant a language exemption, but *only* on the basis of a recent report from a professional psychologist. For this purpose, a special Psychologist's Certification Form (available on www.nui.ie) should be completed and submitted to NUI.

The NUI emphasises that fulfilling minimum entry requirements is just one step towards registration. Students should also familiarise themselves with the admission requirements of the university to which they intend to apply for admission.

Further Resources

BOOKS

	Career Choice 2007, published by Level 3 Publishing and Design 15 Pembroke St., Dublin 2
Carey, D.	The Essential Guide to Special Education in Ireland Primary ABC 2005
Ball, M., Hughes, A. & W. McCormack	Dyslexia, an Irish Perspective Blackhall Press 2006
Dyslexia Association of Ireland	All Children Learn Differently, a Parent's Guide to Dyslexia DAI, 1 Suffolk Street, Dublin 2.
Duddy J. and R. Keane	The Student Yearbook and Career Directory; The Student Yearbook Ltd, Shancroft, O'Hanlon Lane, Malahide
Gilroy, D.E. and T.R. Miles	Dyslexia at College Routledge, 1996
Gilsenan, B.	The Essential Parents' Guide to the Secondary School Years Primary ABC 2004
Hornsby, Dr. B	Overcoming Dyslexia Optima, 1984
King, F.	Special Education in Irish Classrooms Primary ABC 2006
McPhillips, T.	The Learning Support Teacher: a Practical Handbook Blackrock Education Centre 2003

Ott, P. *How to Detect and Manage Dyslexia*
Heinemann 1997

Pollock, J. and E. Waller *Day-to-day Dyslexia in the Classroom*
Routledge,1994

Pumfrey, P. and R. Reason *Specific Learning Difficulty (Dyslexia)*
Challenges and Responses
Routledge 1991

West, T.G. *In the Mind's Eye*
Prometheus Books, 1991

USEFUL WEB ADDRESSES

www.ahead.ie	Association for Higher Education Access and Disability
www.bdadyslexia.org.uk	British Dyslexia Association
www.buzanworld.com	Mindmaps
www.cao.ie	Central Applications Office
www.dyslexia.ie	Dyslexia Association of Ireland
www.education.ie	Department of Education and Science
www.examinations.ie	State Examinations Commission
www.failte.ie	Hotel and Catering courses
www.fetac.ie	Further Education and Training Awards Council
www.homeworktips.about.com	Study plans

www.ldpride.net	Multiple intelligence questionnaire
www.nfq.ie	National Framework of Qualifications
www.ncse.ie	National Council for Special Education
www.ncte.ie	National Centre for Technology in Education
www.qualifax.ie	National careers database
www.scoilnet.ie	Websites for schools, information on careers.
www.sess.ie	Special Education Support Service
www.skillsireland.ie	Expert Group on Future Skills Needs
www.skoool.ie	Study notes for school subjects.

Index